THE SOUL
AND ITS MECHANISM

BOOKS BY ALICE A. BAILEY

Initiation, Human and Solar
Letters on Occult Meditation
The Consciousness of the Atom
A Treatise on Cosmic Fire
The Light of the Soul
The Soul and Its Mechanism
From Intellect to Intuition
A Treatise on White Magic
From Bethlehem to Calvary
Discipleship in the New Age — Vol. I
Discipleship in the New Age — Vol. II
Problems of Humanity
The Reappearance of the Christ
The Destiny of the Nations
Glamour: A World Problem
Telepathy and the Etheric Vehicle
The Unfinished Autobiography
Education in the New Age
The Externalisation of the Hierarchy
A Treatise on the Seven Rays:
  Vol. I — Esoteric Psychology
  Vol. II — Esoteric Psychology
  Vol. III — Esoteric Astrology
  Vol. IV — Esoteric Healing
  Vol. V — Rays and Initiations

THE SOUL
AND ITS MECHANISM

The Problem of Psychology

BY

ALICE A. BAILEY

LUCIS PUBLISHING COMPANY
New York

LUCIS PRESS, LTD.
London

COPYRIGHT © 1930 BY LUCIS TRUST
COPYRIGHT © RENEWED 1958 BY LUCIS TRUST

First Printing, 1930
Sixth Printing, 1973 (First Paperback Edition)
Eleventh Printing, 2002

ISBN No. 0-85330-115-8
Library of Congress Catalog Card Number: 31-995

The publication of this book is financed by the Tibetan Book Fund which is established for the perpetuation of the teachings of the Tibetan and Alice A. Bailey.

This Fund is controlled by the Lucis Trust, a tax-exempt, religious, educational corporation.

The Lucis Publishing Company is a non-profit organisation owned by the Lucis Trust. No royalties are paid on this book.

This title has been translated into Dutch, French, German, Greek, Italian, Portuguese, Russian and Spanish. Translation into other languages is proceeding.

LUCIS PUBLISHING COMPANY
120 Wall Street
New York, NY 10005

LUCIS PRESS, LTD.
Suite 54
3 Whitehall Court
London SW1A 2EF

MANUFACTURED IN THE UNITED STATES OF AMERICA
By Fort Orange Press, Inc., Albany, NY

Dedicated
With my grateful love
to
ALICE E. DUPONT ORTIZ

CONTENTS

	PAGE
FOREWORD	9

CHAPTER I.
Introduction 13

CHAPTER II.
Modern Theory as to the Glands and Human Behaviour 30

CHAPTER III.
The Theory of the Etheric or Vital Body .. 54

CHAPTER IV.
The Nature of the Soul and Its Location .. 72

CHAPTER V.
Oriental Teaching as to the Soul, Ether and Energy 92

CHAPTER VI.
The Seven Centres of Force 109

CHAPTER VII.
Conclusion 128

APPENDIX 154

BIBLIOGRAPHY 158

INDEX 163

"It is easy to show that in the interaction between body and soul there lies no greater riddle than in any other example of causation, and that only the false conceit that we understand something of the one case, excites our astonishment that we understand nothing of the other."

RUDOLF HERMANN LOTZE

"The meaning which descends from the central hope of the self envelops the body; it becomes a city of meanings, and not merely a city of cells. Its organs are no mere facts, but symbols, perilous and profound. It becomes as a whole an object of value, of beauty or deformity, of grace and mechanism, of an implicit philosophy; and attitudes of pride and shame, the infinite interest of art, the versatile significance of the dance, all become intelligible. Posture, gesture, and a million subtle expressive changes of color and tension become the immediate indeliberate manifestations of an inner play. Poetry and morality, religion and logic, regain their seat in our members as well as in our minds, and the world recovers the concrete unity of which our analyses threatened to despoil us."

Self, Its Body and Freedom
By WM. E. HOCKING, p. 97.

FOREWORD

Our attitude toward the philosophical and psychological thought of the East is, for the most part, one either of undiscriminating awe or of equally undiscriminating distrust. It is a pity that this is so. The worshippers are as bad as the distrusters. Neither advance us toward a fair appraisal of that large body of Eastern thinking which is so curiously different from our own and yet, as one discovers after a while, is so fundamentally the same in its essential quest.

It is this undiscriminating attitude which is no doubt to blame for the well nigh entire omission of Eastern thought from our philosophical and psychological books,—this, and another thing. The East has its own idioms which are difficult for the West to understand. Untranslated, they make Eastern writing seem a strange jargon either of confused poetizing or of self-mystification.

Mrs. Bailey, in this book, has done the great service of bringing a critical mind to bear upon Eastern thought, a mind ready to recognize that Eastern, precisely like Western thought, can lay no claim to a finality of wisdom. She does not come with awe-inspiring garb and gesture, bidding the Westerner relinquish his crude inadequacies to embrace a mysterious doctrine all the more wonderful because, to him, it may seem absurd. She says, in effect: "This Eastern thought has the significance of a research into the deeper problems of existence. It is not necessarily better than the Western. It is different. It starts from another angle of approach. Both East and West have specialized in their thinking. Each, therefore, has the virtue of its own sincerity and its own peculiar penetration. But specialization has its value only as it leads to an ultimate integration. Is not the time ripe for bringing East and West together in this profoundest region of the life of each of them, the region, namely, of their philosophical and psychological thinking?"

If for no other reason, this book is significant as an attempt, not only to interpret East to West and West to East, but to bring the two trains of thinking into the harmony of a single point of view. Whether she has successfully achieved the integration remains for the reader to decide. But the attempt is a notable one and should bear fruit in a more intelligent approach to both types of thought.

What gives this book its especial significance, however, is the unique comparison which the author makes between the Western study of the glands and the Eastern study of the "centers." The Western philosopher, Spinoza, long ago noted the indisseverable parallelism of what he called body and mind in the life of the Absolute and in the life of those expressions of the Absolute that we call individuals. If such a parallelism exists, one will expect to find, for every outer manifestation, the inner, or psychic force that thus manifests itself. Hitherto we have taken that assumption of inner and outer only in the most general way. This book, by centering, in the main, on the study of the glands, that are the pace-makers, so to speak, of our personality, presents the body-mind relation not only in a way unexpectedly rich in suggestion for a more adequate training of the individual, but in a way that opens up fascinating possibilities of further research. In the West, we speak of the thyroid or the adrenals altogether in terms of their physiological behavior. Is there likewise a psychic counterpart of this behavior? It seems a queer question to ask and one that at first blush would be scoffed at by the physiological scientists. And yet, unless we are hardened dogmatists who have not yet emerged from the darkness of nineteenth century materialism, we do speak of the psychic counterpart of that physiological organ we call the brain. Why not, then, the psychic counterparts of the thyroid, adrenals, and the rest?

If we pursue this question to its logical end, we shall doubtless learn to extend our thought of what the psychic life of the individual is far beyond the rather naive intellectualistic point which regards that life as centering solely in the brain.

I am holding no brief for the tentative conclusions reached by the author of the book. The particular conclusions may need modification or even rejection. But that the author has opened up new possibilities which may eventually lead to physiological and psychological research that will be of profound significance I have no doubt whatever. The book is not only challenging but singularly illuminating. It will come as a surprise to the Western mind, but with the surprise will, I think, be mingled a very real admiration for processes of Eastern thinking with which we, in the West, are altogether too unfamiliar.

H. A. OVERSTREET

New York City
May 1930

THE SOUL AND ITS MECHANISM

THE PROBLEM OF PSYCHOLOGY

Chapter I

INTRODUCTION

Three desires prompt the writing of this book: the desire to bring together the materialistic or external psychology and the introspective or internal psychology, and, secondly, looking past scientific psychology to the larger realm of race thought and race psychology, the desire to harmonize the materialistic West and the introspective East, and finally to show that all these conflicting aspects are but facets of the one truth and that, together, they constitute the one Reality.

These desires grow out of the present position of psychological teaching in the world. There are today two dominant types of psychology, and Will Durant, in "The Mansions of Philosophy," has well summarised them as follows:

"There are, as we have seen, two ways of studying man. One begins outside with the environment, and considers man as a mechanism of adjustment; it reduces thought to things and 'mind' to 'matter,' and issues in the disguised materialism of Spencer and the behaviorism of Watson. . . . The other way begins within; it looks upon man as a system of needs, impulses, and desires impelling him to study, to use, and to master his environment; it would love to reduce things to thought, and matter to mind; it starts with the 'entelechy' of Aristotle (who held that an inner purpose determines every form), and issues in the vitalism of Bergson and the pragmatism of William James." [1]

Dr. W. B. Pillsbury believes this twofold system involves a needless duplication:

"If the behavioristic theory is retained it means that we must have two psychologies, an external and an internal, a psychology viewed from the outside and one viewed from the inside. This seems at the best an unnecessary complication." [2]

Recognising this duplex situation, and agreeing with Dr. Pillsbury that two lines of interpretation are unnecessary, I am convinced of the possibility of fusing the two into a third, a single unit. I seek, therefore, to present an hypothesis to prove the correctness of the mechanistic school, and the equally correct position of the school of introspectionists, and I seek also to show that both schools are necessary to account for all the facts, and that each is really complementary to the other. Thus we may establish a third or composite school,

---
[1] Durant, Will, *The Mansions of Philosophy*, p. 257.
[2] Pillsbury, W. B., Dr., *The History of Psychology*, p. 298.

Introduction

based upon the exact knowledge of the Occident and the introspective wisdom of the Orient.

In considering these two schools of psychology, it is evident that modern psychology is largely materialistic and the most popular school entirely so. A study of the latest books on psychology, emanating from the many and varied schools in Europe and America, shows that the majority are primarily concerned with endorsing or rejecting the mechanistic philosophy of the Behaviouristic School. If they are not thus occupied they are presenting another form of a materialist psychology. Dr. Wolfgang Köhler in *Gestalt Psychology* says, for instance:

"It is the layman's belief that in general, he himself directly feels *why* at one time he has one attitude, and later on another; also that, for the most part, he knows and understands directly *why* he is inclined to do one thing in a certain particular situation and *why* a definitely different thing under subsequent different conditions. In his view, then, he is experiencing directly and truly much of that dynamical context, the development of which constitutes mental life. Opposed to this belief and altogether foreign to it, we have the view of most learned psychologists at the present time. From their viewpoint, one is inclined to do one thing now and then another, because, in the first instance, certain nerve paths are most available, and, in the second instance, certain other paths are most open. Fortunate those people in whom the most permeable nerve paths in practice are usually the right and appropriate ones!" [3]

---
[3] Köhler, Wolfgang, *Gestalt Psychology*, p. 349.

All is, however, in a state of confusion, and, as has been said by Will Durant—"Psychology has hardly begun to comprehend, much less to control, human conduct and desire; it is mingled with mysticism and metaphysics, with psycho-analysis, behaviorism, glandular mythology and other diseases of adolescence." [4]

Psychology is wandering in that borderland of the unseen which we dignify with the words *energy*—whether nervous, atomic or vital,—*force,* etheric vibrations, and *electric currents and charges* and *the freely floating force* of the psychologists, to which has been given the name *libido.* All the sciences seem to be converging on this same no-man's land, on the indefinable. Perhaps the veil, when lifted, will reveal to us the promised land of man's dreams and aspirations. A spirit of uncertainty and expectancy is paralleling the certainties and cold facts of modern science. It is almost as if mankind were standing before the curtain in a cosmic proscenium, waiting for it to rise and reveal the next act, in which humanity can participate intelligently. It is a humanity with a long past, much gained experience and accumulated knowledge, which stands thus waiting, but it is also a humanity which realises that it may be called upon to take part in a revelation and a development wholly unexpected, and for which its present equipment and understanding of life may prove inadequate.

---

[4] Durant, W., *Mansions of Philosophy,* p. 376.

Meanwhile in this cosmic proscenium, and in the approach to truth through various lines, science has arranged the known facts and is deducing the next possible development and is proceeding in its many branches and activities upon hypotheses which, correct or incorrect, merit experiment and test. Voicing what should be the attitude of mind for students in all fields of human knowledge, Bertrand Russell says: "What we need is not the will to believe, but the wish to find out, which is the exact opposite." [5]

The best type of mind to cope with this scientific situation today is that which is sceptical, yet willing to be convinced; agnostic, yet determined to investigate fairly; questioning, yet open to conviction when supposed facts are proved to be favourable of demonstration; and above all broadminded, realising that only in the formulated truths of the many can the one Truth be known. Only the small mind, the little man, is atheistical, dogmatic, destructive in criticism, static, with back turned to the light, and to the new day.

This searching, enquiring, scientific type of mind and of investigation is especially appropriate in psychology, the oldest branch of knowledge in the world, and yet the youngest to enter the realm of true scientific study. Only a willingness to consider the field as a whole, and not a particular school alone, only by reserving opinion until more is known, will the investigator avoid the dan-

---
[5] Russell, Bertrand, *Sceptical Essays*, p. 157.

gers of one whose vision is limited, who sees only isolated points but never the panorama in which they lie, and who deals in fractions and decimals without ever achieving an integral unit.

One of the most hopeful signs of the time is the growing understanding of the Oriental point of view, and the tendency to investigate it. The psychology of our two hemispheres is so widely different, the approach to truth so dissimilar, that only lately have students considered the possibility of their fundamental unity, and that a new outlook on man and his environment may emerge out of the fusion of the Eastern and Western interpretations of life. Old interpretations may fail, yet ancient truths will stand: old misconceptions may be recognised as misleading, but reality will radiate clearer light and beauty. From the union of our different sciences, thought and deductions, a new psychology may emerge based on the comprehension, so familiar to the West, of the structure which man uses, and the comprehension, so familiar in the East, of the energy or spirit with which man animates and directs his structure. These—the structure and the motivating energy—are not antagonistic but mutually interdependent. They have an essential unity.

Western psychology concerns itself primarily with the structure, with the tangible objective universe and with the reaction of objective man to that world. It deals with man as an animated body; it emphasises the mechanics of his nature,

Introduction 19

and the instrument he uses. It is therefore mechanistic and deals only with that which can be subjected to tests and experiment. It investigates the body and accounts for the emotions and the mentality, and even for what it calls the soul, in terms of the body. Durant points out this position in the following words: "As for the Self or Soul, it is merely the sum total of the hereditary character and the acquired experiences of the organism."[6] It explains various types and temperaments in terms of the mechanism. Louis Berman sums up this position in his interesting book as follows:

"The most precious bit of knowledge we possess today about Man is that he is the creature of his glands of internal secretion. That is, Man as a distinctive organism is the product, the by-product, of a number of cell factories which control the parts of his make-up, much as the different divisions of an automobile concern produce the different parts of a car. These chemical factories consist of cells, manufacture special substances, which act upon the other cells of the body, and so start and determine the countless processes we call Life. Life, body and soul emerge from the activities of the magic ooze of their silent chemistry precisely as a tree of tin crystals arises from the chemical reactions started in a solution of tin salts by an electric current.

Man is regulated by his Glands of Internal Secretion. At the beginning of the third decade of the twentieth century, after he had struggled, for we know at least fifty thousand years, to define and know himself, that summary may be accepted as the truth about

---
[6] Durant, Will, *The Mansions of Philosophy*, p. 75.

himself. It is a far-reaching induction, but a valid induction, supported by a multitude of detailed facts." [7]

Thus Western psychology emphasises the physical and seen and, in its chosen field, is scientific. It is constitutionally opposed to the idle and dreaming speculations of the visionary mystic. The result of its efforts has been to isolate a body of facts which do effectively embody the truth about man, his behavior and equipment. This knowledge should be invaluable in producing a better mechanism through which a finer race can function.

Western psychology, in its more extreme schools, is actively deterministic for it relates all feeling, thinking and activity to the functioning of the physical cells and the bodily organs. Freewill is therefore largely ruled out in favor of the organism, the nervous apparatus, and of the endocrine system. The following quotations bear this out.

"Watson in his 'Psychology from the standpoint of a Behaviorist,' would teach that 'emotion is an heredity pattern-reaction involving profound changes of the bodily mechanism as a whole, but particularly of the visceral and glandular systems" (p. 195); and that 'thought is the action of language mechanisms' (page 316); is 'highly integrated bodily activity and nothing more' (p. 325); and that 'when we study implicit bodily processes we are studying *thought*.' By this Watson does not mean to identify thought with the correlated cortical activity of the brain—not at all;

---
[7] Berman, Louis, M.D., *The Glands Regulating Personality*, p. 26.

but with all the bodily processes that are involved, implicitly and explicitly, in the production of spoken, written and sign language—the muscular activity of the vocal apparatus, diaphragm, hands, fingers, eye-movements, etc. (p. 324).[8]

"Psychology studies the world with man left in it, i.e., it studies experience as dependent upon the nervous system, whereas physics studies experience as though existing independently of the nervous system. Psychology should, therefore, be classified with the general sciences as a discipline laying bare the general traits of mind, where mind is defined as 'the sum-total of human experience considered as dependent upon a nervous system.' . . . Psychology studies the total environment viewed as existing only at the moment when it affects the (human) nervous system, whereas physics studies the total environment viewed as existing beyond the moment when it affects the (human) nervous system.[9]

"Thirdly, the faith of the mechanist implies two assumptions which we must carefully distinguish; for one of them may be false, though the other be true. These two assumptions are (1) that all processes in the world are fundamentally of one kind only (2) that all these processes are of the kind commonly assumed by the physical sciences in their interpretations of inorganic nature; namely mechanistic, or strictly determined, and therefore strictly predictable, events."[10]

Dr. Rubin says, "the physical appearance of the individual, his psychic traits, or what might be called the chemistry of his soul, are demon-

---
[8] Prince, Morton, *Psychologies of 1925*, p. 208.
[9] Hunter, Walter S., *Psychologies of 1925*, p. 95.
[10] McDougall, William, *Psychologies of 1925*, p. 303.

strated in a great measure by the character and amount of the internal secretions of his various glands."[11]

Some schools go so far to deny consciousness altogether and regard it (the Eastern investigator would say they rightly regard it) as inherent in matter. Dr. Leary says, "Consciousness characterizes nerves as vibration characterizes other forms of matter."[12]

Thus it is defined elsewhere as "a complex integration and succession of bodily activities which are closely related to or involve the verbal and gestural mechanisms and hence most frequently come to social expression."[13]

Watson warns his readers that they "will find no discussion of consciousness and no reference to such terms as sensation, perception, attention, will, image and the like. These terms are in good repute, but," he says, "I have found I can get along without them both in carrying out investigation and in presenting psychology as a system to my students. I frankly do not know what they mean nor do I believe that anyone else can use them consistently."[14]

Finally we are told that "When psychology has become quite divorced from *psyche* and gets in bed with living beings we shall be able to throw the word 'consciousness' into the discard—along

---

[11] Rubin, Herman H., M.D., *Your Mysterious Glands*, p. 54.
[12] Leary, Daniel H., Ph.D., *Modern Psychology: Normal and Abnormal*, p. 116.
[13] Hunter, Walter S., *Psychologies of 1925*, p. 91.
[14] *Psychologies of 1925*, p. 201, footnote.

with 'mind' and 'memory.' Human behavior then will be on a scientific basis and not a branch of literature, or philosophic or religious speculation. 'Mind' will give way to personality, 'consciousness' in general to specific exhibitions of learned behavior, and 'memory' to the calling out of some part of the individual's striped or unstriped muscle-tissue organization." [15]

This intensely materialistic trend of Western psychology is the more surprising when we remember that, according to its derivation, psychology is the 'logos' or word of the psyche or soul.

The West, however, has its dissenting voices. There is the introspective school of psychology, more frequently called the introspectionist, and also the mentalist. They admit the fact of consciousness and assume a conscious entity. Dr. Leary defines these groups as follows:

"The introspectionist is interested in consciousness, awareness, awareness of awareness, the self, the 'I' images, and all sorts of other things that the behaviorist of strict training and rigid technology scorns, ignores and denies. . . . The introspectionist turns his attention inwardly; remembers, compares mentally, derives data from self-communion, asks others to do the same; the behaviorist theoretically treats the human animal the same as he would any lower form of life, and observes merely the overt and objective responses the animal makes in much the same manner as would be used by the physicist or chemist in observing the reactions of bodies or compounds in their labo-

---

[15] Dorsey, George A., *Why We Behave Like Human Beings*, p. 333.

ratories. Furthermore, the subjective school is apt to be ultra-rational and systematic; the behavioristic more empirical and pragmatic. . . .

"The mentalists insist that psychical activity is not the mere reflection of physical activity; that over and above the body and the brain there is something different, on a different level, call it mind, spirit, consciousness, what you will. Thought is not the functioning of matter. The materialists on the other hand, while differing among themselves, would hold just the reverse, namely, that all is physical, and that all human conduct, be it thinking, feeling, emotions, muscle activity or nerve activity, is all the functioning of physical, material cells, and that without such structure there can be no activity at all. Whatever acts is physical, however it acts. On the one hand we have an informing power or spirit using the structure of the physical body; on the other we have structure as the basis, solely and indispensably, of function, however complex, however delicate, however noble that functioning may be in terms of morals or religion." [16]

The introspectionists and mentalists have not, however, demonstrated their point scientifically, and the position of these schools is still further weakened by the many diverse groups into which psychology is divided. Dr. Hocking, of Harvard, says:—

"True, psychology does not speak with a single voice. There is dynamic psychology and purposive psychology, Gestalt psychology and reaction psychology, Freudian psychology, structural psychology, behavioristic psychology, and various other schools. They pro-

---

[16] Leary, Daniel B., Ph.D., *Modern Psychology: Normal and Abnormal*, pp. 6-7.

Introduction

duce different portraits of the self. But the composite of them has a distinctly physiological cast; and we may take behaviorism as the pure instance, because it is the extreme instance, of this character." [17]

A broad and general division is outlined for us by Dr. Prince as follows:

> "Psychologists are divided into three camps—the self-psychologists, the selfless psychologists and the middle grounders. The first group maintain that the content of every conscious process includes a self—an awareness of self, a self-consciousness. Hence that all consciousness is a consciousness or awareness of something by a *self*.
>
> "The second group, the selfless ones, claim to be unable to find any self, or consciousness of self by introspection; deny its reality and hold that mental processes function without any such reality. The 'I' and the 'You' are merely compulsory expressions required by the necessities of language." [18]

Western psychology in the mass is clearly materialistic. It is mechanistic, thriving in an age of machines and machinery.

The position of the Western mechanistic psychologist is, therefore, almost impregnably strong, for it is based upon known truths and demonstrated facts. He can prove his position and cite his cases, and his knowledge of the mechanism of man which he claims is the entire man, is based upon experiment and tests, with objective and tangible results.

---
[17] Hocking, Wm. E., *Self, Its Body and Freedom*, pp. 17, 18.
[18] Prince, Morton, *Psychologies of 1925*, p. 223.

Against this materialistic psychology, the criticism which emerges immediately is the almost exclusive consideration that the Western Psychologist gives to subnormal, deficient, and pathological cases. The super-normal, the genius, and the so-called highly spiritual individual have been neglected, and much that is beautiful, essential and true to the average man is explained away. Had He been subjected to psycho-analysis, Christ would no doubt have found Himself neatly tabulated and classified, as suffering from a "Jehovah complex" and regarded as subject to hallucinations. Yet the type of structure that He used, and the quality of the "consciousness characterizing His nervous system" was such that He has set His mark upon the ages. How can such a structure again be duplicated? What can be done to reproduce a similar mechanism?

Modern psychology is only at the threshold of its career, and Walt Whitman visions the greater field thus:

> "Hurrah for positive science! Long live exact demonstration!" . . .
> Your facts are useful, and yet they are not my dwelling,
> I but enter by them to an area of my dwelling" [19]

In sharp contrast with the Western School is the Eastern one of which the introspectionists and mentalists in the West, though arising independ-

---

[19] Whitman, Walt, *Leaves of Grass*, p. 10.

ently, are but a hazy reflection. Eastern psychology deals with that which it claims lies back of the form. It is spiritual and transcendental. It assumes a soul and a spirit and all its deductions and conclusions are based on this premise. It fully admits the form and the structure, but lays the emphasis upon the one who uses the form and the energy with which he drives it forward. It is the psychology of life and energy.

From time immemorial this has been the thought of the East, and it is clearly pictured in that venerable scripture of India, *The Bhagavad Gita:*

"The Supreme Spirit, here in the body, is called the Beholder, the Thinker, the Upholder, the Taster, the Lord, the Highest Self.

"Illuminated by the power that dwells in all the senses, yet free from all sense-powers, detached, all supporting, not divided into powers, yet enjoying all powers.

"Without and within all beings, motionless, yet moving, not to be perceived is That, because of its subtlety, That stands afar, yet close at hand. XIII:22, 14, 15.

"These temporal bodies are declared to belong to the eternal lord of the body, imperishable, immeasurable. II:17.

"They say the sense powers are higher than objects; than the sense powers, emotion is higher; than emotion, understanding is higher; but higher than understanding is He. III:42."

Thus Oriental psychology deals with the cause, with the creator, with the self, whether that self is the human divine self, functioning in its own little world of mental, emotional and physical activities, or the great Self, in whom all lesser selves live and move and have their being. It claims its great Demonstrators, and has produced those claiming to know the Self, and through that knowledge to be in touch with the subjective Self, with the Over Soul. These claims, they state, can be substantiated and proven by any who will study their methods and submit to their special training. In the sphere of the energising Self, of the spirit behind and beyond, their position is as clear as that of the Western psychologist in the realm of the energised form.

The defects of the two systems are plain and produce deplorable results in each case. The West emphasises the mechanism, and its tendency is towards the denial of the soul and of a motivating intelligent power. For it, man is but dust of the ground and into his nostrils was never breathed the spirit of God. The East recognises the physical but scorns it, and, in so doing, becomes responsible for the miserable physical conditions of the Orient. Serious as these defects are, is it not true in this field also that in union there is strength?

If the Self exists—and this must be demonstrated—and is the conscious divine Soul, can it not be aware of the physical plane as well as of its divine affiliations? If it is the dominant energy, producing all manifestation—and this too must be proved—cannot that energy be adapted to the structure which it uses in such a wise and significant manner that the best results may be achieved? Cannot the scientific knowledge of the West about the form, and the accumulated and inherited wisdom of the East about the nature of the Soul be brought together intelligently so that a perfect expression of the Soul may be produced through the medium of the mechanism? Cannot matter reach upwards towards mind and Soul and Spirit —call it what you will—and cannot Spirit, assisting that urge upward, perfect the vehicle through which it demonstrates, and thus shine more radiantly?

It is in this hope that I write—the hope of combining the materialistic and introspective psychologies, and of harmonising the West and the East, and so indicate that in their union lies strength and reality.

Chapter II

THE GLANDS AND HUMAN BEHAVIOUR

The study of the glands is in its infancy. Throughout the literature on this subject, one finds statements to the effect that little is known, and that the inner essence—technically called "hormones"—of any particular glandular secretion has not yet been discovered, and that mystery veils the subject. It is true that the secretions of certain glands have been discovered, and that even in common parlance one hears of the thyroid gland and of the administration of thyroid extract in certain cases, but the secretions of most glands are unknown or have only partly been isolated.

Under these circumstances, an intelligent layman, even if not scientifically trained in medicine or in academic psychology, but armed with patience and a stout dictionary, need not hesitate to venture upon the subject of glands and their secretions and effects, and, after diligent study of the available material, to survey the field and report on it. Such a survey, in fact, may be of real value to the general public by supplying it with a ready summary of an important branch of inquiry. It may also be of substantial help even to the trained exponent, not merely enabling him to ascertain the impression which the technical literature makes on others, but especially because a fresh mind, unhampered with scientific data, frequently gains a better perspective of the whole field. This would be particularly so if the one, so surveying and reporting, has long been versed in the race-old beliefs and age-long convictions of the East on the general subject of psychology.

In considering the endocrine system, it is not my intention to describe it in its ordinary physiological terms and effects, such as its relation to the growth of the body, to the hair, heart, blood and organs of generation. All this can be gathered out of any medical book, even those published in the last century. Rather is it my intention to ascertain what advanced and modern investigators, medical men and psychologists, infer from a study of the glands, and what they judge their effects to be on human behaviour, and to check the claims, so often made, that the mysterious internal secretions are responsible for man's actions, emotions and mentality—in short, for the man himself. Understand the glands, they say, and behold the man.

In considering glands in this sense, I shall quote largely from the available books, not merely because one is then more likely to speak as having authority, but also because one thus reflects the given view more freshly and vividly. A partial bibliography will be found at the close of this book.

These books, and the trained investigators as a whole, use a terminology that staggers the general reader. The secretion of the thyroid gland, for example, has been labelled as "tri-iodo-tri-hydro-exygindole-propionic acid!" As far as possible, I shall avoid such playful expressions.

Before considering the glands themselves, it is well to decide what we understand by "psychology." In the West at least, it has abandoned its derivative meaning, already given, of the logos or law, of the psyche or soul. A recent and clear definition is given by Dr. Leary:

"The science of human behavior in the largest sense of the word behavior, the sense which includes all that human beings do, all that human beings have. In this sense of behavior it is the behavior of the whole, integrated personality which is under investigation.

"Psychology deals with the organism as a whole, as an integrated and orientated individual in contact with other individuals in a complex external environment, partly physical and partly social, in short, as a personality.

"The behavior of human beings, psychologically speaking, . . . reduces to physiological facts and findings, in turn to those of the field of biology, then to those of bio-chemistry, then to chemistry in general and then, inevitably, to physics as the science of matter in motion." [1]

Psychology, therefore, is the science of the activity of man, as a living organism, in the en-

---

[1] Leary, Daniel B., *Modern Psychology: Normal and Abnormal*, pp. 10, 14, 18.

vironment in which he finds himself—the science of the interplay between man and that environment. It is the science of human conduct, but not in the ethical sense of right or wrong conduct. It is the science of human behaviour, of personality. But what is there behind this behaviour? Hocking says, "The self is indeed a system of behavior. But it is a system of *purposive behavior emerging from a persistent hope*. The kernel of the self is its hope." [2]

This hope that life may be made something that is greater than it has ever hitherto been, is indeed a persistent hope—we know, however, that if it is to be realised, we ourselves must help to bring about that realisation. Hence the purposive behaviour of which Hocking speaks.

In this field of human behaviour and personality, there are three main factors. There is, first, the environment. This is much more than a mere present fact, or set of facts, or a mere passive stage upon which the drama is played. It has been defined as "all that is not the organism, whether cultural, social, physical, or what-not, present in fact or in record." [3] There is, secondly, the human apparatus, especially the response apparatus which we shall presently discuss in greater detail. There is, finally, conduct, or the result of the interrelation between the environment and the response apparatus, and, given a certain environment and

---
[2] Hocking, Wm. E., *Self, Its Body and Freedom*, p. 46.
[3] Leary, Daniel B., *Modern Psychology: Normal and Abnormal*, p. 45.

a certain response apparatus, certain lines of conduct, it is claimed, are inevitable—the interplay of these three results in human behaviour.

Our concern here is naturally with the second main factor, the response apparatus.

In that apparatus, certain aspects of the mechanism warrant closer attention than others, namely the nervous system, and the system of ductless glands, which two systems are found functioning in close co-ordination in the human frame.

It is through the nervous system, perhaps the most intricate and wonderful part of the human structure, that we contact our environment, the external world, and are adapted to function in it. Through this system we become aware of the tangible, and through the network of nerves, plus the spinal cord and brain, we become aware of information ceaselessly conveyed to us. Messages are carried along the millions of telegraph lines of our nerves to the central power house of our brain, and are then transformed in some mysterious way into information. To that information we respond: a reverse activity is instituted and we are galvanised into action.

Along with this display of incoming and outgoing nervous energy there are parallel activities in the system of ductless glands (and the muscular system) and the interlocking of activity is so great that, unless the ductless glands are functioning normally, there will be no adequate response

Glands and Human Behaviour

to the information telegraphed and no transformation of one type of energy into another.

The whole response apparatus, and the mechanics of the case, have been summed up in the following terms:

"An organism is a transforming device which changes the incoming energy of the environment, received through the receptors, into outgoing energy in the form of the work of the muscles and glands and, at the same time, as transforming device, also transforms itself in terms of these and other, inwardly originating stimuli, both sets of stimuli and both outputs of energy co-operating in the complete act or behavior of the organism." [4]

The nervous system and muscles may be loosely described as the physical response apparatus, and the means by which physical response to the environment is made, but the nervous system and the ductless glands as the intelligent and emotional response apparatus, and the means by which actual response is made.

It is claimed that this latter inter-action between the apparatus and the environment produces conduct and behaviour, that feeling and thought activity have their seat in the endocrine system, and that even the nature of man is thus accounted for!

"It is probably true," continues Dr. Leary, "that, in the long run, when present speculation has been replaced by more adequate and better

---
[4] Leary, Daniel B., *Modern Psychology: Normal and Abnormal*, p. 33.

grounded knowledge, we will find the seat of temperament in, or in connection with, the ductless glands." [5]

Dr. Rubin says "we are now rapidly coming to believe that all we are and all we may ever hope to be, depends very largely upon whether or not we have been born with normal ductless glands." [6] And Dr. Leary says, "The emotions are more nearly concerned with interoceptors and unstriped muscles and ductless glands" than instincts are.[7] Dr. Cobb tells us:

". . . only three and a half grains of the thyroid secretion stands between intelligence and idiocy. It is a gruesome thought to realize that the absence of one chemical can result in a failure of development of the mind and body of an individual." [8]

Dr. Cobb also tells us in his Introduction that:

"The action of the glands in determining the bodily build is indisputable; and the mental outlook—the 'behavior complexes'—of the individual appears to depend on the physical well-being; and the physical well-being undoubtedly depends upon the successful action and interaction of the various glandular secretions. . . .

"Although we are as yet only on the fringe of the subject, we have advanced sufficiently to realize that, just as certain patterns are formed in the body by a

---
[5] *Ibid.*, p. 189.
[6] Rubin, H. H., *Your Mysterious Glands*, p. 10.
[7] Leary, Daniel B., *Modern Psychology: Normal and Abnormal*, p. 61.
[8] Cobb, I. G., M.D., *The Glands of Destiny*, p. 5.

particular arrangement of the ductless glands, so does the mind receive its quota from the same source." [9]

Professor J. S. Huxley in a recent lecture says, "It seems clear that temperament even more important than pure intellect in achieving success, is largely an affair of the balance of the various glands of internal secretion—thyroid, pituitary, and the rest. It may well be that the applied physiology of the future will discover how to modify temperament." [10]

In regard to this matter of temperament, Dr. Hocking remarks:

"There is not the slightest reason to doubt the broad fact of the profound effect on temperament exercised by the glands of internal secretion, such as the thyroid or the interstitial glands or the adrenals. The stimulation of certain of these glands, or the injection of their products, or feeding therewith, may produce changes which would once have been thought miraculous. By administering thyroxin a cretin may be brought to something resembling normality; if the dosage is stopped he returns to his original condition. If the dosage is increased, unfortunately, neither he nor anyone is raised from normality to genius; we only produce another form of abnormality. And so far, no chemical discoveries justify any bright hopes of improving the human normal. There are, indeed, certain drugs which make an individual feel like a genius, but unless the results are judged under the same influence they are strangely disappointing. We must, therefore, not build at once too high hopes for

---

[9] Cobb, I. G., M.D., *The Glands of Destiny*, pp. 3, 6.
[10] Ibid., pp. 11, 12.

the future of mankind on these discoveries. But there is a genuine sense in which the soul has its chemistry, and 'a deficiency of iodine will turn a clever man into an idiot.' " [11]

The consideration, therefore, of the ductless glands and of their effect not only on physical structure, but on conduct as well, is of vital importance. What then are the glands? And, especially, what are the ductless glands often mentioned? Dr. Cobb tells us:

"Glands may be divided into two main groups, those which are concerned with the drainage system—the lymphatic glands—and those which *secrete* products for use in the bodily work. The lymphatic glands do not concern us here. The second group, whose duty is to contribute fluids which, acting in concert with each other, control and regulate the bodily processes, consist of two subdivisions.

"The first of these contain glands with ducts, down which they discharge their contents. The second possess no ducts, and their secretions are absorbed directly into the blood stream. These are known as the *ductless glands,* or 'endocrine organs' and their products have been called internal secretions. The term 'endocrinology' has been applied to the study of the glands of internal secretion." [12]

The word "endocrine" it may be noted is from the Greek word "krinein," meaning "to separate." Dr. Rubin says:

---
[11] Hocking, W. E., *Self, Its Body and Freedom*, pp. 58, 59.
[12] Cobb, I. G., M.D., *The Glands of Destiny*, p. 1.

Glands and Human Behaviour

"These ductless glands or organs of secretion are often referred to as the 'endocrine glands.' Their secretions are absorbed directly into the blood, and into the streams of nutrient lymph—the body, it would appear, thereby dispensing its own drugs.

"These secretions contain the 'hormones' or chemical messengers of the organism which excite some of the most marvelous reactions known in physiology. In fact, it has been stated that hormones are to physiology what radium is to chemistry." [13]

This system of endocrine glands forms a unit functionally, working in the utmost co-operation and interdependence. Dr. Berman tells us, "The body mind is a perfect corporation. Of this corporation the glands of internal secretion are the directors. . . . Behind the body, and behind the mind is this board of governors." [14] All the glands, in fact, work in unison. They are known to correlate their activity, to balance each other, and through their united effect, it is claimed, to make a man what he is.

They form, in fact, a close interlocking system with functions and organisms clearly distinct from those of other systems within the mechanism of the human frame. The blood system and the nervous system pursue their own activities, but are closely linked to the endocrine system. The blood acts mysteriously as the carrier of the peculiar hormones of the different glands, and the nervous sys-

---
[13] Rubin, H. H., M.D., *Your Mysterious Glands*, pp. 8, 9.
[14] Berman, Louis, M.D., *The Glands Regulating Personality*, pp. 96, 97.

tem seems more specifically related to the psychical development incident to the normal, or abnormal, functioning of the endocrine glands.

From this discussion of the endocrine system we come naturally to the question: What, then, are the ductless glands, one by one?

Beginning with the head, and working downwards, there are seven glands of special importance to be listed. These are:

Name	Location	Secretion
1. Pineal gland	Head	Unknown
2. Pituitary—	Head	
anterior		Unknown
posterior		Pituitrin
3. Thyroid	Throat	Thyroxin
4. Thymus	Upper Chest	Unknown
5. Pancreas	Solar Plexus region	Insulin
6. Adrenals—	Behind the kidneys	
cortex		Unknown
medulla		Adrenalin
7. Gonads	Lower Abdomen	Of the testes and ovaries

Thus we have distributed over the head and torso a network of important glands, which, it is claimed, physiologically govern the structure, growth and chemical changes of the body, and, psychologically, are responsible for the emotional reactions and the thought processes of the human being. Hence, they would be the producers of his

---

Since this chapter was written, experiments with the ductless glands have continued. Details given here are not final or conclusive but the basic postulates of the Author remain untouched. F.B.

Glands and Human Behaviour 41

qualities, good and bad, of his behaviour and conduct of affairs, and of his very character.

We shall now consider the seven glands mentioned, but confining our discussion to their mental and psychic effects.

1. The pineal gland—location, head—secretion, unknown.

The pineal gland is cone-shaped, about the size of a pea, and is in the center of the brain in a tiny cave behind and above the pituitary gland which lies a little behind the root of the nose. The pineal gland is attached to the third ventricle of the brain. It contains a pigment similar to that in the retina of the eye, and also collections of what have been called "brain sand particles." Dr. Tilney says:

> "Numerous attempts have been made to determine what function, if any, the pineal body possesses. Is it indispensable to life, or does it play some role important to a particular phase of metabolic activity? We may perhaps concede that this organ does possess a function in man and in most mammals. It is not improbable that this function is particularly determined by an internal secretion, a secretion, however, which is certainly not indispensable to life. The exact influence of the pineal secretion is still obscure." [15]

It has also been suggested that this gland regulates our susceptibility to light, that it has a definite effect upon the sex nature, that it is related to brain growth and that its active functioning

---
[15] Tilney, Frederick, M.D., *The Pineal Gland*, pp. 537, 542.

causes intellectual precocity as is clearly indicated in the historic case discussed below. This gland has also been called the third eye, and the eye of the Cyclops. Beyond these facts or conjectures, investigators frankly say they know nothing, and experiments have produced little information. In the experiment of feeding pineal gland extract to children and to defectives the response was nothing when the subject was over fifteen years of age, and contradictory in all other cases, so deduction was impossible.

Until a few decades ago scant attention was paid to the pineal gland. Then came the case, noted by Dr. Berman, in which a child was brought to a German clinic suffering from eye trouble and headaches. He was five years old and very mature, and apparently had reached the age of adolescence. He was abnormally bright mentally, discussing meta-physical and spiritual subjects. He was strongly group-conscious and only happy when sharing what he had with others. After his arrival at the clinic, he rapidly grew worse and died in a month. An autopsy showed a tumor of the pineal gland.[16]

As will be seen later, this historic case has a special interest in view of the conclusions of Oriental philosophers.

Most of the books note that the pineal gland is stated by ancient philosophers to be the seat of the soul, and Descartes is frequently quoted as

---
[16] Berman, Louis, M.D., *The Glands Regulating Personality*, p. 89.

saying, "In man, soul and body touch each other only at a single point, the pineal gland in the head."

In the ancient belief that the pineal gland is the seat of the soul and in the fact apparently established that the pineal gland is a distinctive gland of childhood and atrophies later, is there not, perhaps, some real connection, some indication of hidden truth? Children have a ready belief in God and recognition of Him. Christ said, "The Kingdom of Heaven is within you" and "Except ye become as little children ye shall not enter into the Kingdom of Heaven."

One is mindful, too, of Wordsworth's "Ode on Intimations of Immortality from Recollections of Early Childhood."

> "Our birth is but a sleep and a forgetting;
>   The soul that rises with us, our life's star,
>   Hath had elsewhere its setting
>   And cometh from afar;
>   Not in entire forgetfulness,
>   And not in utter nakedness,
>   But trailing clouds of glory do we come
>   From God who is our home:
> Heaven lies about us in our infancy!
> Shades of the prison-house begin to close
>   Upon the growing Boy,
> But he beholds the light, and whence it flows,
>   He sees it in his joy.
> The youth, who daily farther from the East
>   Must travel, still is Nature's priest,
>   And by the vision splendid
>   Is on his way attended;

> At length the Man perceives it die away,
> And fade into the light of common day."

Oriental philosophy confirms this possible connection between the pineal gland and the soul.

2. Pituitary—location head—secretion of anterior gland unknown, secretion of posterior, pituitrin.

Interest in the pituitary gland has been evidenced for centuries but until the late eighties so little was known about it that it was regarded as an organ of external secretion. It is really two glands in one. It is about the size of a pea and lies at the base of the brain a short distance behind the root of the nose.

This gland has been called "nature's darling treasure," being cradled in a niche, like a "skull within a skull." As most of the glands do, in some form or other, it has a close relation to sex, and is also related to such periodic phenomena as sleep and sex epochs. We are told that it is a gland of continued effort, of energy consumption, and is essential to life. It is believed to stimulate the brain cells and to have a "direct and important bearing upon the personality." We are also informed that insufficient pituitary development causes, or at least accompanies conspicuous moral and intellectual inferiority, and lack of self-control; but that with a good pituitary development there will also be pronounced mental activity and endurance. It seems to have a very close connection with our emotional and mental qualities.

The pituitary, as we have said, is really two glands in one. The secretion of the post-pituitary is pituitrin.

"The post-pituitary governs the maternal-sexual instincts and their sublimations, the social and creative instincts. . . . It might be said to energize deeply the tender emotions. . . . For all the basic sentiments (as opposed to the intellectualized self-protective sentimentalism), tender-heartedness, sympathy and suggestibility, are interlocked with its functions."

The secretion of the ante-pituitary is unknown.

"The ante-pituitary has been depicted as the gland of intellectuality. . . . By intellectuality we mean the capacity of the mind to control its environment by concepts and abstract ideas." [17]

Dr. Berman also adds, "Mental activity is accompanied by increased function of the ante-pituitary, if intellectual, or of the post-pituitary, if emotional." [18]

From a study of these comments, it becomes apparent that the personality qualities—emotions, whether we mean maternal instincts shared with all animals, love of one's fellowmen, or love of God,—are regarded as largely dependent upon the condition of the pituitary gland, as is also the ability to intellectualise.

Approaching the problem from a different angle, the student of the Eastern wisdom proves the relative correctness of all these inferences.

---
[17] Berman, Louis, M.D., *The Glands Regulating Personality*, p. 178.
[18] Ibid., p. 236.

3. Thyroid—location, throat—secretion, thyroxin.

Of the thyroid gland, more is known than of the pineal gland or the pituitary body, and from the standpoint of Eastern wisdom, this was to be expected. This gland is found astride the neck, above the wind-pipe, close to the larynx, and is a very large gland. It was once a sex gland, is frequently called the "third ovary," is always involved in ovarian cases. In the lower vertebrates it is clearly connected with the ducts of the sexual organs, but in the march of evolution upwards, "that relationship is lost, the thyroid migrates more and more to the head region, to become the great link between sex and brain." [19] We are told also that it is the great differentiator of tissues, and has anti-toxic power, preventing poisoning and increasing resistance to poison.

Above everything else, however, the thyroid gland is the controller of the metabolism of energy. It has been called the efficient lubricator of energy transformation, and is the great catalyst of energy in the body. It controls the speed of living and is the keystone of the endocrine system. It is indispensable to life.

Through the work done with subnormal people, deficients and idiots, investigators have come to the conclusion that, in the words of Dr. Berman:

"Without thyroid there can be no complexity of thought, no learning, no education, no habit-formation,

---
[19] Berman, Louis, M.D., *The Glands Regulating Personality*, p. 46.

Glands and Human Behaviour

no responsive energy for situations, as well as no physical unfolding of faculty and function and no reproduction of kind, with no sign of adolescence at the expected age, and no exhibition of sex tendencies thereafter." [20]

We are also told that

"Sensitivity, the ability to discriminate between grades of sensation or acuteness of perception is another thyroid quality. Just as the thyroid plus is more energetic, so is he more sensitive. He feels things more, he feels pain more readily, because he arrives more quickly at the stage when the stimulus damages his nerve apparatus." [21]

The thyroid like the pituitary, has also close connection with the memory.

". . . the pituitary seems to be related to preservation of the memory deposit. . . . The thyroid memory applies particularly to perception and precepts, the pituitary to conception (reading, studying, thinking) and concepts." [22]

4. Thymus—location, upper chest—secretion, unknown.

Of the thymus gland, we know practically nothing, and it is one of the most mysterious of all. Like the pineal gland, it is regarded as a gland of childhood, but both as yet baffle investigation.

The thymus gland is situated in the chest, covers the upper portion of the heart, and, perhaps, has relation to nutrition and growth. It seems to be

---
[20] Ibid., p. 55.
[21] Ibid., p. 180.
[22] Berman, Louis, M.D., *The Glands Regulating Personality*, p. 182.

connected with the irresponsible nature of children, and, when over-functioning in adult years, produces the irresponsible man or woman, and the amoral people.

5. Pancreas—location, solar plexus region—secretion, insulin.

Most of the information given in connection with the pancreas is strictly physiological, and, therefore, out of place here. Suffice it to say, however, that it lies in the abdomen and is close to the solar plexus (which is the brain of the instinctual animal nature) and is closely concerned with the "mobilization of energy for physical and mental purposes. It has two secretions, both insulin, one concerned with the digestive processes and the other known to be vital to the metabolism of sugar. Without sufficient sugar for the cells, no muscle work or nerve work—essentials in the struggle for existence—are possible." [23]

6. Adrenals—location behind the kidneys—secretion of the cortex adrenals unknown, of the medulla adrenals adrenalin.

The adrenal glands are each of them dual and are situated on both sides of the abdomen, astride and back of the kidneys. They are concerned with general growth, and the growth of the brain cells. The adrenal cortex secretion (to which no name has been given) is one source of the internal secretions producing maturity.

---
[23] Ibid., p. 93.

The adrenal glands, however, are primarily the glands of combat. They produce that immediate and active response which men exhibit in times of danger or anger, and their secretion is stimulated in times of emergency. Pain, rage and fear have a definite effect upon the discharge, and we are told, "all the evidence points to its medulla as the secretor of the substance which makes for the phenomena of fear, and to its cortex as dominant in the reactions of anger." [24]

Also:

"Courage is so closely related to fear and anger that all are always associated in any discussion. Courage is commonly thought of as the emotion that is the opposite of fear. It would follow that courage meant simply inhibition of the adrenal medulla. As a matter of fact the mechanism of courage is more complex. One must distinguish animal courage and deliberate courage. Animal courage is literally the courage of the beast. As noted, animals with the largest amounts of adrenal cortex are the pugnacious, aggressive, charging kings of the fields and forests. The emotion experienced by them is probably anger with a sort of blood-lust, and no consideration of the consequences. The object attacked acted like a red rag waved at a bull—it had stimulated a flow of the secretion of the adrenal cortex, and the instinct of anger became sparked, as it were, by the new condition of the blood. In courage, deliberate courage, there is more than instinct. There is an act of volition, a display of will. Admitting that without the adrenal cortex such courage would be impossible, the chief credit for courage

---

[24] Berman, Louis, M.D., *The Glands Regulating Personality*, p. 76.

must be ascribed to the ante-pituitary. It is the proper conjunction of its secretion and that of the adrenal cortex that makes for true courage. So it is we find that acts of courage have been recorded most often of individuals of the ante-pituitary type." [25]

7. Gonads—location, lower abdomen—secretion, that of male testes and female ovaries.

The gonads or interstitial glands are the sex glands of external secretion, but are known to have an internal secretion also. Their gross secretion is the medium for reproduction. It is unnecessary to dwell at length upon the effects of the gonads on personality. The sex impulse and its various subsidiary effects, both physical and psychical, are well recognized and much studied, and this study, largely of perversions and inhibitions, has proved of paramount importance to the understanding of humanity. Some psychologists relate all human reactions—physical, emotional and mental—to sex and sex alone, and, back of every extreme position, we know there lies a substratum of truth. Others regard sex as playing an important part, but not as responsible for the entire story. The Eastern wisdom offers an interpretation which warrants consideration and which will appear when we consider the force centers and their relation to the glands.

Of all the foregoing, and of many books and articles on the subject, the following may be given as a brief summary.

---

[25] Berman, Louis, M.D., *The Glands Regulating Personality*, p. 177.

Glands and Human Behaviour 51

The whole subject is in an experimental stage, and much remains to be done. Clearly, however, there is a close relationship between the glands and a similarity of function, and most of them have to do with the metabolism of the body and with growth, and all of them seem closely related to sex life. Finally, they determine, apparently, the type and temperament of the personality.

Experimental as the science is, man seems to have been psycho-analysed and understood at last. Those elusive and intangible processes, called emotions and mental concepts, are accounted for in terms of matter. To the glands and to the nervous system, and to the poor or good development and functioning of man's apparatus of contact and response, is ascribed all that he is. A saint can be made into a sinner and the sinner into a saint, and this merely by increasing or decreasing certain internal secretions. Thus a man is no better, no worse, than the equipment with which he comes into the world and his mechanism is the sum total of him. He can improve it or misuse it, but the apparatus is the determining factor. Free-will is eliminated and immortality denied. The best a man can do is so to act that he is happy and, also, to shoulder the responsibility of building better bodies in order that the next generation can manifest better psychically.

Whether we agree with those conclusions or disagree, we must at least admit that, with the mechanism the object of all study, it should eventually be possible to ascertain the laws and methods by which perfect bodies may be constructed which, in turn, can be the instruments through which a perfect psychic nature can function.

But are all these conclusions as to the endocrine glands, in fact correct? Has man, in outline, been classified and labelled, and does there remain only the filling of blanks in the general outline? Who can say? But to my mind the answer lies in two questions or groups of questions, the one primarily a matter of the individual, and the second all-embracing.

As for the individual, are glands and glandular functions primary causes, or are they merely effects or instrumentalities? Is there not, in truth, something greater which lies beyond? Is there not in each of us a soul which functions through the whole physical and psychic mechanism? Was not St. Paul, in short, right in saying that man has a natural body and a spiritual body, and in implying that the glory of the natural is one, and the glory of the spiritual another?

And as for the second and broader question, is a mere mechanism the be-all and end-all of existence, and our only guiding star the perfecting of that mechanism? Then, indeed, "let us eat and drink, for tomorrow we die." Is it not that there is not only a finer self in us—call it spirit, soul, or what you will,—but does it not, itself form a part of a transcendent whole—call it God as religion does, or Oversoul as Emerson does, or by any other name—but in any case a transcendent whole, the glory and radiance of which surpass all understanding? Shall we never be at-one with That, and meanwhile the longing for that at-one-ment lead us onward? Shall this corruptible never put on incorruption, or this mortal never put on immortality? Shall death never be swallowed up in victory?

For answers to these questions, let us turn to the Wisdom of the East.

Chapter III

THE THEORY OF THE ETHERIC BODY

The Oriental psychologist starts with that which the Occidental regards as hypothetical. He lays the emphasis upon the spiritual nature of man, and believes that the physical nature itself is the result of spiritual activity. He asserts that all that is objectively seen is but the outward manifestation of inner subjective energies. He regards the entire mechanics of the cosmos and of man as effects, and believes the scientist is dealing only with effects. His position may be summed up as follows:

First: There is nothing but energy, and it functions through a substance which interpenetrates and actuates all forms, and which is analogous to the ether of the modern world. Matter is energy or spirit in its densest form, and spirit is matter in its most sublimated aspect.

Second: As all forms are interpenetrated by this ether, every form has an etheric form or etheric body.

Third: As the tiny atom has a positive nucleus, or positive nuclei, as well as negative aspects, so in every etheric body there are positive centers of force in the midst of negative substance. The human being too has an etheric body which is positive to the negative physical body, which galvanises it

Theory of the Etheric or Vital Body

into activity, and which acts as its coherent force, holding it in being.

Fourth: The etheric body of man has seven main nuclei of energy through which various types of energy flow, producing his psychical activity. These nuclei are related to the cerebro-spinal system, and the base of this psychical activity, or the seat of the soul nature, is situated in the head. The governing principle therefore is in the head and from this center the entire mechanism should be directed, and energised through the medium of the other six force centers.

Fifth: Only certain centers are now functioning in man and the rest are quiescent. In a perfect human being all the centers will function fully and produce perfect psychical unfoldment and a perfect mechanism.

This Oriental emphasis upon spiritual energy and the Occidental emphasis upon the structure or mechanism, it will be seen, accounts fully for the psychical nature of man, both in its higher and in its lower aspects.

To unite the Eastern or vitalistic conception, and the Western or mechanistic conception, and so bridge the gap between them, it is necessary to establish the fact of the existence of the etheric body.

The Oriental system is abstruse and intricate, and defies summarisation. Still, some brief introduction must be made and the following outline is therefore given. It is incomplete, but if it gives an intelligible survey of the field, however brief, it will serve its purpose.

In giving this outline, we shall make positive statements instead of continually repeating that "the Eastern psychologist believes" or "the Orientalist states" or similar expressions. It is enough to recognise once and fully that to the Western mind it must be presented as an hypothesis, to be submitted to test, to stand proved or fall disproved.

With this introduction we proceed to outline the Eastern theory.

There is a universal substance, the source of all, but so sublimated, so subtle that it is truly beyond the real grasp of human intelligence. In comparison with it, the most delicate fragrance, the dancing radiance of sunbeams, the crimson glory of the sunset, are gross and earthly. It is "a web of light," forever invisible to human eye.

The key word "substance" with its suggestion of materiality is a misnomer. It is helpful however, to reduce this word to its Latin roots:—"sub" under and "sto" to stand. So, substance is that which stands underneath, or underlies. The spelling, or misspelling "sub-stans" is more indicative and suggestive.

Subtle and fugitive as this universal substance is, yet in another sense it is denser even than matter. If we could conceive of an agent outside of universal substance—an hypothesis contrary to all fact and possibility—and if such an external agent attempted to compress universal substance, or in some

Theory of the Etheric or Vital Body

other way affect it from without, then substance would be found denser than any known material.

Inherent in substance, and a perpetual counterpart of it, is life, incessant life. Life and substance are one and the same, one and forever inseparable, but different aspects however, of the one reality. Life is as positive electricity, substance negative. Life is dynamic, substance static. Life is activity or spirit, and substance form or matter. Life is the father and begets, substance is the mother and conceives.

In addition to these two aspects of life and substance, there is still a third. Life is theoretical or potential activity, and needs a field of operation. Substance furnishes this and in the union of life and substance, there flames forth active energy.

Thus we have a single reality, universal substance;—but at the same time a co-existent duality, —life and substance, and at the same time, a co-existent trinity, life, substance, and the resultant interaction which we call consciousness or soul.

The entire manifested world arises from energy (and the co-factors substance and consciousness). All that is seen, from the tiniest grain of sand to the widest sweep of starry heaven, from an African savage to a Buddha or a Christ, all are outgrowths of energy. Matter is energy in its densest or lowest form; spirit is this same Energy in highest or most subtle form. So matter is spirit descending and debased; spirit, conversely, is matter ascending and glorified.

In taking on density, energy takes on, or descends into, seven degrees or planes. Man exemplifies three. He has his physical body, his emotional mechanism and his mind-body, and consequently functions on three planes, or is awake on three, the physical, the emotional and the mental. He is on the threshold of the recognition of a fourth and higher factor, the Soul, the Self, and will next awaken to that realisation. The three higher planes require no comment in this elementary discussion.

In addition to seven planes, each plane has seven subplanes. We shall discuss only the seven subplanes of the lowest or physical plane.

Three sub-planes of the physical are known to every school-boy,—the solid, liquid and gaseous, for example, ice, water and steam. In addition there are four subtler planes, or rather four different types of ether. These four are co-existent with each of the three well known sub-planes, and interpenetrate them.

The physical body of man is no exception. It, too, has its etheric counterpart, its etheric body. This is positive, while the dense physical body is negative. The etheric body is the cohesive factor, and maintains the physical body in life and being.

The etheric counterpart, whether of man or of any physical thing, is of the universal substance, of universal life, and of universal energy. It partakes of all of these. But it is not self-sufficient or independently existing. It draws upon the reser-

Theory of the Etheric or Vital Body 59

voir of universal energy, and in it the etheric counterpart lives and moves and has its being. Energy is thus functioning through the etheric.

This is true of man also. The universal energy functions through his etheric body. And as man exists on seven planes, so the etheric body has seven points of contact with energy,—but as only three planes are active, and four dormant, so only three force centers are fully developed and four as yet undeveloped. Of this, more later.

In harmonising the two schools, the question naturally arises, does Western Science corroborate the Eastern theory?

No less a scientist than Sir Isaac Newton accepts the universal medium of ether without question. In the last paragraph of his Principia, he says:

"And now we might add something concerning a certain most subtle spirit which pervades and lies hid in all gross bodies; by the force and action of which spirit the particles of bodies mutually attract one another at near distances, and cohere if contiguous; and electric bodies operate to greater distances, as well repelling as attracting the neighboring corpuscles; and light is emitted, reflected, refracted, inflected, and heats bodies; and all sensation is excited, and the members of animal bodies move at the command of the will, namely by the vibrations of this spirit, mutually propagated along the solid firmaments of the nerves, from the outward organs of sense to the brain, and from the brain into the muscles. But these are things that cannot be explained in few words, nor are we furnished with that sufficiency of experiments which is required to an accurate determination and demonstration of the laws by which this electric and elastic spirit operates." [1]

Thus it can be argued from the above that Newton recognised the facts of the etheric body, underlying all forms, including the human.

As Newton is not of this century or the last, let us turn to a recent edition (1926) of the *Encyclopaedia Britannica*. The following discussion is given under the heading of "ether."

"Whether space is a mere geometrical abstraction, or whether it has definite physical properties which can be investigated, is a question which in one form or another has often been debated. As to the parts which are occupied by matter, that is by a substance which appeals to the senses, there has never been any doubt; and the whole of science may be said to be an investigation of the properties of matter. But from time to time attention has been directed to the intervening portions of space from which sensible matter is absent; and this also has physical properties, of which the complete investigation has hardly begun.

"These physical properties do not appeal directly to the senses, and are therefore comparatively obscure; but there is now no doubt of their existence; even among those who still prefer to use the term space. But a space endowed with physical properties is more than a geometrical abstraction, and is most conveniently thought of as a substantial reality, to which therefore some other name is appropriate. The term used is unimportant, but long ago the term ETHER was invented; it was adopted by Isaac Newton, and is good enough for us. The term ether there-

---

[1] Burtt, Edwin Arthur, Ph.D., *Metaphysical Foundations of Modern Physical Science*, p. 275.

fore connotes a genuine entity filling all space, without any break or cavity anywhere, the one omnipresent physical reality, of which there is a growing tendency to perceive that everything in the material universe consists; matter itself being in all probability one of its modifications. . . .

"Thus an ether is necessary for the purpose of transmitting what is called gravitational force between one piece of matter and another, and for the still more important and universal purpose of transmitting waves of radiation between one piece of matter and another however small and distant they be. . . .

"The properties of the ether are not likely to be expressible in terms of matter; but, as we have no better clue, we must proceed by analogy, and we may apologetically speak of the elasticity and density of the ether as representing things which, if it were matter, would be called by those names. What these terms really express we have not yet fathomed; but if, as is now regarded as very probable, atomic matter is a structure in ether, there is every reason for saying that the ether must in some sense be far denser than any known material substance. . . .

"Matter therefore is comparatively a gossamer structure, subsisting in a very substantial medium. . . ." [2]

These views are amplified by other scientists of note.

Writing in the 17th century, Henry More, the Cambridge Platonist as quoted by Dr. Burtt said:

"Whence, I ask if it be unworthy of a philosopher to inquire of a philosopher if there be not in nature an incorporeal substance, which, while it can impress on any body all the qualities of body, or at least most

---

[2] *Encyclopaedia Britannica,* 13th Edition: Article: Ether.

of them, such as motion, figure, position of parts, etc. ... would be further able, since it is almost certain that this substance removes and stops bodies, to add whatever is involved in such motion, that is, it can unite, divide, scatter, bind, form the small parts, order the forms, set in circular motion those which are disposed for it, or move them in any way whatever, arrest their circular motion, and do such similar further things with them as are necessary to produce according to your principles light, colours, and the other objects of the senses. ... Finally, incorporeal substance having the marvelous power of cohering and dissipating matter, of combining it, dividing it, thrusting it forth and at the same time retaining control of it, by mere application of itself without bonds, without hooks, without projections or other instruments; does it not appear probable that it can enter once more in itself, since there is no impenetrability to frustrate it, and expand itself again, and the like."

In discussing Henry More, Dr. Burtt goes on to say:

"In this passage More extends his reasoning from the conclusion of an incorporeal substance in human beings to the assumption of a similar and greater incorporeal substance in nature as a whole, for he was convinced that the facts of science showed nature to be no more a simple machine than is a human being." [3]

Also writing in the 17th century, Robert Boyle brought forward the same hypothesis and ascribed two functions to ether, to propagate motion by successive impacts and to be a medium through which

---
[3] Burtt, Edwin Arthur, Ph.D., *Metaphysical Foundations of Modern Physical Science*, pp. 131-132.

Theory of the Etheric or Vital Body 63

curious phenomena manifested, such as magnetism, Boyle said:

"That there may be such a substance in the universe, the asserters of it will probably bring for proofs several of the phenomena I am about to relate; but whether there be or be not in the world any matter that exactly answers to the descriptions they make of their first and second elements I shall not here discuss, though divers experiments seem to argue that there is an ethereal substance, very subtle and not a little diffused." [4]

Coming again to modern times Sir William Barrett said:

"The universe presents us with an assemblage of phenomena—physical, vital, and intellectual—the connecting link between the worlds of intellect and matter being that of organized vitality, occupying the whole domain of animal and vegetable life, throughout which, in some way inscrutable to us, movements among the molecules of matter are originated of such a character as apparently to bring them under the control of an agency other than physical, superseding the ordinary laws which regulate the movements of inanimate matter, or in other words, giving rise to movements which would not result from the action of those laws uninterfered with; and therefore implying, on the very same principle, the origination of force." [5]

The Eastern teaching regards the vital body as the intermediary between the physical and the intellectual: it acts as the agency of the mind in a human being and of the Universal Mind in a solar

---
[4] Ibid., pp. 182, 183.
[5] Barrett, Sir William, *On the Threshold of the Unseen*, p. 274.

system, and it is interesting to note in this connection Sir William Barrett's threefold enumeration of "physical, vital and intellectual."

Sir Oliver Lodge, though often criticised for his views as to communication between the living and the dead, is, in matters of pure science, in the front rank of this age. He says:

> "What about the Ether which holds the atoms together, the welding ether which is essential to the characteristic configuration of a body—which is as essential as the matter itself?
>
> "We do not usually attend to the ether aspect of a body; we have no sense organ for its appreciation, we only directly apprehend matter. Matter we apprehend clearly when young children, but as we grow up we infer the Ether, too, or some of us do. We know that a body of characteristic shape, or indeed of any definite shape, cannot exist without the forces of cohesion—cannot exist therefore without the Ether;—meaning by the Ether now, not the whole, but the unmaterialized part of it, the part which is the region of strain, the receptacle of potential energy, the substance in which the atoms of matter are embedded. Not only is there a matter body, there is also an ether body: the two are coexistent." [6]

He takes up the same subject again in an article which appeared in *The Hibbert Journal* and presents some most interesting and suggestive conclusions, as follows:

> "Light is an affection of the ether. Light is to ether as sound is to matter. . . . Subject to all the laws of

---
[6] Lodge, Sir Oliver, *Ether and Reality*, pp. 161, 162.

Theory of the Etheric or Vital Body 65

time and space, fully amenable to the laws of energy, largely the source of terrestrial energy, governing all the manifestations of physical forces, at the root of elasticity and tenacity and every other static property of matter, the ether is just beginning to take its rightful place in the scheme of physics: ...

"Electric charges, composed of modified ether, are likely to prove to be the cosmic building material. ... There is the great bulk of undifferentiated ether, the entity which fills all space and in which everything material occurs. A duality runs through the scheme of physics—matter and ether—.

"All kinetic energy belongs to what we call matter, whether in the atomic or the corpuscular form; movement or locomotion is its characteristic. All static energy belongs to the ether, the unmodified and universal ether; its characteristics are strain and stress. Energy is always passing to and fro from one to the other—from ether to matter or vice versa—and in this passage is all work done.

"Now, the probability is that every sensible object has both a material and an etherial counterpart. One side only are we sensibly aware of, the other we have to infer. But the difficulty of perceiving this other side—the necessity for indirect inference—depends essentially and entirely on the nature of our sense organs, which tell us of matter and do not tell us of ether. Yet one is as real and substantial as the other, and their fundamental joint quality is co-existence and interaction. Not interaction everywhere and always, for there are plenty of regions without matter—though there is no region without ether; but the potentiality of interaction, and often the conspicuous reality of it, everywhere prevails and constitutes the whole of our purely mundane experience."

In a supplementary note to the article, he says:

"Ether belongs to the physical frame of things, no one supposes it be a psychic entity; but it probably subserves psychical purposes, just as matter does. Professors Tait and Balfour Stewart surmised a psychic significance for the ether of space so long ago as 1875, and treated it from a religious point of view in that much criticized book *The Unseen Universe*. And that great mathematical physicist, James Clerk Maxwell, concluded his article "Ether" in the ninth edition of the *Encyclopedia Britannica* with an expression of faith, not indeed in this speculation, about which he evinced great caution, but in the real existence of a supersensuous universal connecting medium, and in the probability of its having many unsuspected functions." [7]

Dr. Sajous, Professor of Endocrinology in Pennsylvania University asserts his belief in this universal medium in the following terms:

"It seems plain that the need of a primary intelligent and co-ordinative creative medium such as the ether asserts itself on all sides. . . .

"The ether, as interpreted by scientists, meets all these conditions and is the only medium known to science that is capable of doing so. It is invisible, permeates all matter and pervades all space by wave motion, without limit in the universe. It offers practically no resistance to radiant energy, even to light from the sun and the most distant stars discovered. It is the medium which transmits 'radio' waves, wireless telegraphy waves, Becquerel rays, X- or Roentgen rays, etc.

---
[7] Lodge, Sir Oliver, *Ether, Matter and the Soul*, Hibbert Journal, January, 1919.

"The ether is endowed with creative power in space and on earth. . . . The ether of space, therefore, builds solar systems as it does matter, with co-ordination and intelligence, and endows all chemical elements it forms with the properties they are known to possess. . . ." [8]

Dr. Joad of Oxford University pictures for us the activity of this vital force, of the 'livingness' animating matter and shows the relationship between life and form. He comes close indeed, to the Eastern theory of the etheric counterpart and the energy functioning through it.

"The Life Force. Let us suppose that in the first instance the universe was purely material. It was chaos, deadness and blankness, without energy or purpose, and devoid of life. Into this inorganic universe there is introduced at some stage or other, and from some source unexplained, a principle of life, and by life I mean a something which is not expressible in terms of matter. At first blind and stumbling, a purely instinctive thrust or pulse, it seeks to express itself by struggling to achieve an ever higher degree of consciousness. We may conceive the ultimate purpose of the life force to be the achievement of complete and universal consciousness, a result which can only be secured by the permeation of the whole universe with life and energy, so that beginning as a world of 'matter' it may end as a world of 'mind,' or 'spirit.' With this object it works in and through matter, infusing and permeating matter with its own principle of energy and life. To matter so infused we give the name of a living organism. Living organisms are to be re-

---

[8] Sajous, Chas. E. de M., M.D., ScD., LLD., *Strength of Religion as Shown by Science,* pp. 152, 153.

garded in the light of the tools or weapons which the life force creates to assist it in the accomplishment of its purpose. Like the universe itself, each living organism is formed of a substratum of matter which has been animated by life, much as a length of wire may be charged with an electric current. It is a current of life which has been insulated in a piece of matter.

"The life force is far from being all-powerful. It is limited by the matter which it seeks to overcome, and its methods are experimental, varying according to the stage of evolution which, in the persons of the organisms created by it, it has succeeded in reaching. Different types of beings best serve its purpose at different stages." [9]

Will Durant, doubtless the most widely read and popular author on philosophical subjects, says:

"The more we study matter the less we see it as fundamental, the more we perceive it as merely the externality of energy, as our flesh is the outward sign of life and mind. . . . In the heart of matter, giving it form and power, is something not material, possessed of its own spontaneity and life; and this subtle, hidden and yet always revealed vitality is the final essence of everything that we know. . . . Life is first, and within; matter, coeval with it in time and inextricable from it in space, is second to it in essence, in logic, and in significance; matter is the form and visibility of life. . . .

"The life is not a function of the form, the form is a product of the life; the weight and solidity of matter are the result and expression of intra-atomic energy, and every muscle or nerve in the body is the moulded instrument of desire." [10]

---

[9] Joad, C. E. M., B.A., *Mind and Matter,* pp. 178, 179.
[10] Durant, Will, *Mansions of Philosophy,* pp. 66, 67, 80, 81.

Theory of the Etheric or Vital Body

These books and scientists show that the Eastern doctrine of an etheric body, the medium of a vital force, of energy or life, is not the vague dream of a mystically inclined people, but is regarded as a fact in nature by many practical minded Occidental investigators.

In summarising our ideas we might formulate them as follows:

Behind the objective body lies a subjective form constituted of etheric matter and acting as a conductor of the life principle of energy, or prana. This life principle is the force aspect of the soul, and through the medium of the etheric body the soul animates the form, gives it its peculiar qualities and attributes, impresses upon it its desires and, eventually directs it through the activity of the mind. Through the medium of the brain the soul galvanises the body into conscious activity and through the medium of the heart all parts of the body are pervaded by life.

This theory has a close correspondence to the animistic theory of the West and will be defined later. The term animism has sufficed up to the present, but is likely to be superseded by that of "dynamism," owing to the developments taking place within the human consciousness itself. Man, being now a fully self-conscious entity and the personality being now integrated and functioning, the time has come when he can, for the first time, demonstrate conscious purpose and directive will.

The three states of man's nature, referred to

earlier in this chapter,—physical, sentient and mental,—form a co-ordinated unity for the first time in the history of the race. The directing self, therefore, can now take control, and, through the mind, acting on the vital or etheric body and having its point of contact in the brain, drive its instrument into fully controlled expression, and subsequent creative activity. Thus will emerge what Keyserling calls the "deeper Being," He says:

"The next question is whether and how it is possible to develop deeper Being. When we speak of the Being of a man in contradistinction to his ability, we mean his vital soul; and when we say that this Being decides, we mean that all his utterances are penetrated with individual life, that every single expression radiates personality, and that this personality is ultimately responsible. Now such a penetration can actually be achieved where it does not already exist. It is possible, thanks for the fact that man as a being possessing a mind and a soul represents a Sense connection within which his consciousness moves freely. He is free to lay the emphasis wherever he pleases; according to the 'place' thus stressed the psychic organism actually shifts its centre, and thus actually obtains a new centre of Being. Therefore, if theoretical inquiry shows that it depends upon the centering of consciousness, whether the centre of a man lies in his Being or at the surface, then it must be practically possible to induce the necessary process of shifting. Hence in principle everybody can succeed in raising his Being; to this end he need only persistently lay the emphasis on his essential Being, persistently demand of himself that he should never utter anything but what is really consistent with his inner Being. Surely the task is a hard one. Its solution is not only a very slow process; it necessitates a specific technique of training." [11]

The possibility of man functioning as a soul, as a synthesis of mechanism, life and purpose, will, I believe, be greatly hastened when the Eastern and Western psychologies are merged and the relationship of the *Glands* to the vital body, with its centers of force, studied and understood. Hocking in this connection, comes to this conclusion:

"There seems reason to hope for a better physical future of the race by the aid of a sound mental hygiene. After the era of the charlatans has gone by, and to some extent by their aid, there appears a possibility of steadily enlarging self-mastery, as the spiritual sense of such discipline as the Yoga joins with the sober elements of Western psychology and a sane system of ethics. No one of these is worth much without the others." [12]

Two points merit discussion, before we pass on to a detailed account of the Eastern teaching as to the force centers. One is a consideration as to the nature of the soul, and the other is an attempt to consider the testimony of the centuries as to the probable location of the soul consciousness.

---
[11] Keyserling, Count Hermann, *Creative Understanding*, pp. 180, 181.
[12] Hocking, Wm. E., *Self, Its Body and Freedom*, p. 75.

Chapter IV

THE NATURE OF THE SOUL AND ITS LOCATION

Throughout the ages the soul has been the subject of discussion, of argument, and of attempted definition. It has been, and still is, the paramount intellectual interest of the ages, and the outstanding theme of all religions and philosophies. From this alone, we may perhaps deduce that the soul is possibly a fact in nature, for the testimony of millennia must have some basis in reality. After the elimination of all conclusions founded on the visions and experiences of hysterics, of neurotics, and of pathological cases, there remains a residue of testimony and a structure of deduction, emanating from sane and reputable thinkers, philosophers and scientists, which evades negation and warrants recognition by humanity.

Dr. Richard Müller-Freienfels says, "To write the history of man's belief in the soul one would have at the same time to write the history of the whole human race."[1]

The problem has been well summarized for us by Professor Ames:

"On the one side was this self or soul, with its thinking; on the other, all the world of objects, other per-

---
[1] Müller-Freienfels, Richard, *Mysteries of the Soul*, p. 24.

The Nature of the Soul and Its Location 73

sons and God. The efforts of wise men for centuries have been to find a way to span the chasm between the self and other objects. But with ideas as events in the head, and things existing outside, there was no sure bridge upon which to make the passage that alone could guarantee that the representations in the head were true to the objects in the outer realm. Upon the two sides of this gulf have been arrayed the armies of philosophers: the idealists upon the side of the self, vainly trying to stretch themselves to reach the reality they have posited as separated from their grasp; and on the opposite side the materialists, striving to ignore the self or to regard it as a phantom, or epiphenomenon, a breath or mist, exuding from the physical world itself. Some, called dualists, assumed the reality of both the psychical and the physical, but allowed each its place and never succeeded in an adequate answer to the question as to how the mind goes out of itself to so different an object, or how the object could be itself and yet be known." [2]

Some definitions of the soul might here have place. They have been gathered out of a vast number. It is noticeable that there is a very remarkable uniformity in definition and exegesis. Webster defines the soul in most interesting terms, and from the standpoint of the Eastern wisdom, with great exactitude.

"An entity, conceived as the essence, substance, or actuating cause of individual life, especially of life manifested in psychical activities; the vehicle of individual existence, separate in nature from the body and usually held to be separable in existence."

[2] Ames, Edward Scribner, Prof. of Philosophy, University of Chicago, *Religion*, pp. 127-128.

As one investigates the different interpretations as to the nature of the soul, three points of view emerge and these have been well summarised for us in Webster's Dictionary:

"First, the soul has been treated as an entity or subject, manifested especially in man's volitional thinking activities; it is the subject of the experience meditated by the body; it is not the mind, but that which thinks and wills.

"Second, the soul is identified with the mind or with conscious experience; this is the usual sense of the word in psychology, and is the general conception of idealists.

"Third, the soul is treated as a function or the sum of the functions of the brain; thus Pierre J. G. Cabanis (1757-1808), taught that the brain secretes thought as the stomach digests food."

Webster adds the following comment which is appropriate in its application to the present trend of world thought:

"Some conceptions, such as that of Fechner, that the soul is the whole unitary, spiritual process in conjunction with the whole unitary bodily process, appear to stand mid-way between the idealistic and materialistic views." [3]

Perhaps, after all, the "noble middle path" which the Buddhist emphasises, holds for the coming generation a way of escape from these extreme positions.

The Egyptians held the soul was a divine ray,

---
[3] *Webster's Dictionary*, Edition of 1923.

The Nature of the Soul and Its Location

acting through a peculiar, fluid-like compound, whilst the Jews regarded it as the vital principle. The Hindus teach that the human soul is a portion of an immutable Principle, the Soul of the World, the Anima Mundi, the all pervading Ether (Akasa) of space. This Ether is simply the conductor of certain types of energy and serves as the interrelating medium between essential spirit and tangible matter.

Pythagoras, who did so much in his day to link the Eastern and Western philosophies, gave the same teaching. In China, Lao-tse taught that the spiritual soul is united to the semi-material vital soul, and between them they animate the physical body. The Greeks, in their turn, held that the soul (with all the mental faculties) was separable from the body, whilst the Romans regarded the soul as a triplicity,—a spiritual soul, an intellectual soul or the mind, and a vital body. Many, such as Theophrastus, regarded it as "the real principle of passion," and

"The Stoics gave currency to a new designation of the animating principle or theory of the vital processes, namely pneuma. . . . With the introduction of the pneuma began that trichotomy of human personality into body, soul and spirit, which has figured prominently in the speculations of theologians. The conception of the soul or psyche . . . became differentiated into two conceptions . . . namely, on the one hand, the vital force of the physiologists, and on the other hand the spirit or immaterial soul of man." [4]

---
[4] Hollander, Bernard, M.D., *In Search of the Soul*, Vol. I, pp. 53-54.

The Stoics therefore emphasised a teaching which is entirely in line with the Oriental philosophy. They bridged the gap therefore between the two hemispheres.

Plato expounded the doctrine of the soul in the following manner:

"He believed the soul to have three parts. One, an immortal or rational part, coming from God; another a mortal, animal or sensitive part, the seat of appetite and sensation, belonging to the body; and a third, lying between these and making their interaction possible—will or spirit—by means of which reason conquered desire. Plants have the lowest part; animals the two lower; but the rational part is exclusively human.

This rational soul he regarded as immaterial and metaphysical in nature, incapable of being perceived by the senses, and only to be grasped by the intellect. The union with the mortal, material and physical body was only a minor incident of its long career . . . Plato thus drew a fundamental distinction between soul and body." [5]

Aristotle regarded the soul as the sum of the vital principles and as being to the body what vision is to the eye. The soul was to him the true Being in the body, and with him Plotinus was in agreement. He regarded the soul as the living sentiency of the body, belonging to a higher degree of being than matter. Tertullian divided the soul into two parts, a vital and a rational principle, as did St. Gregory. Most of the Oriental schools regard

---
[5] Ibid., p. 35.

The Nature of the Soul and Its Location

the soul as the self, the individual, and Christian mysticism is concerned with the elaboration of the teaching of St. Paul, that there dwells in each human being a potentiality which is called by him "Christ in you," and which, through its presence, enables every man eventually to attain the status of the Christ. A close comparison of the Christian and Oriental teachings leads to the conclusion that the terms: Self, Soul, Christ, connote the same state of being or consciousness, and indicate the subjective reality in every man.

The early Christian Fathers were tremendously influenced by Greek ideas as to the Soul, and their teaching was later coloured by Gnosticism and Manicheanism. By them the soul was regarded as light and the body as darkness; light must irradiate the body and eventually be liberated from the body. St. Gregory in the 4th century emphasised the triplicate of body, soul and spirit as did St. Paul. He summed up in his teaching the point of view of the best thinkers of his time, and (quoting Dr. Hollander) taught that:

". . . the Soul has no parts, yet Gregory distinguished nutritive, sensitive, and rational faculties, corresponding to the body, soul and spirit. The rational nature is not equally present in all parts of the body. The higher nature uses the lower as its vehicle. In matter resides the vital power; in the vital dwells sensitive power, and to the sensitive power is united the rational. The sensitive soul is thus a medium, purer than flesh and grosser than the rational soul. The soul thus united with the body is the real source of all activities." [6]

From the 5th century on to the 17th we have the ideas of various schools; of Scholastics, of Arabian philosophers, of Kabbalists, also the philosophers of the Middle Ages, and that notable group of men who brought about the Reformation and Renaissance. They discussed the various theories accounting for the soul, but not much progress was made, for all was gradually tending towards the emergence of modern science, the establishment of modern medicine, and the revelations of the age of electricity. Gradually the form aspect of nature and the laws governing natural phenomena engrossed attention, until speculations as to the soul and its nature were increasingly relegated to the theologians.

In the 17th century, Stahl wrote fully upon the subject of the soul and summarised a great deal of the teaching extant in his time. This has been termed the Theory of Animism. It is the doctrine that the soul is the vital principle, and responsible for all organic development. We speak of the animism of the little evolved races, who personified and worshipped the forces of nature; we recognise the animism outlined by Stahl in the later cycles of our own time as having been always present; we study the modern scientists' teaching as to force, as to energy, as to the atom, and we find that we are

---

[6] Hollander, Bernard, M.D., *In Search of the Soul*, Vol. I, p. 88.

The Nature of the Soul and Its Location

confronted by a world of energies which cannot be negated. We live in a universe animated by forces. Speed, activity, vitality, transportation, the transmission of sound, electrical energy, and many such phrases are the catch-words of today. We speak and think in terms of force.

Stahl summed up the teaching in the following terms:

> "The body is made for the soul; the soul is not made for, and is not the product of, the body. . . . The source of all vital movement is the soul, which builds up the machine of the body, and maintains it for a time against external influences. . . . The immediate cause of death is not disease, but the direct action of the soul, which leaves the bodily machine, either because it has become unworkable through some serious lesion or because it does not choose to work it any longer." [7]

Berkeley's definition of the soul is interesting, for he defines it as a simple, active being, revealed to us through experience.

The modern materialistic psychology which regards the soul as the product of brain activity is perhaps not entirely wrong but is dealing with a secondary demonstration of the vital soul.

Dr. Müller-Freienfels says:

> ". . . we must not regard the body as an atomistic mechanism but rather as the vehicle of a comprehensive vital energy; whereupon the 'body' ceases to be merely matter and is conceived of as being 'animated'."

---

[7] Hollander, Bernard, M.D., *In Search of the Soul*, Vol. I, p. 169.

He goes on to say also:

"And now at last we see a possibility of arriving at a conception of the soul! Let us remember how mankind came to form this conception. Not in order to explain the 'consciousness' (for the 'soul' can exist without consciousness), but in order to make comprehensible that complex continuity of activities which we call life, mankind created the conception of the soul. We have already stressed the fact that in all primitive cultures the 'soul' is by no means identical with the consciousness, and that this equivalence is a late philosophical reservation. As a matter of fact, what primitive man understands by 'soul' is what we today call 'life.' 'Animated' and 'alive' are, as conceptions, completely identical, just as the conceptions 'inanimate' and 'dead' are identical. The Greek word *psyche* does not by any means signify merely consciousness, but can usually be translated simply by 'life,' and similarly, in many cases the German words *Leben* and *Seele*, as the English words 'life' and 'soul,' are interchangeable. . . .

In this, however, we are at one with both the main tendencies of recent philosophy. Even the later materialists had come to admit that the soul is not a substance, but that the psychical processes occur in substance, and they therefore regarded it as equivalent to 'motion.' On the other hand, the conscientialists also regarded psychical processes as 'events' which they had somehow to bring into relation with physical movements.

We accept both these notions. What we call 'soul' is neither an extended 'substance' nor a thinking 'substance'; it is not a 'substance' at all, but a highly complicated event, a continuity of effects, which reveals itself on the one hand in the building up of the body, and on the other in the consciousness.

The Nature of the Soul and Its Location

Nevertheless, this doctrine of ours, which does not divide the universe into substance and consciousness, but places a connecting-link between the two, which on the one hand reveals itself materially, but is also the hypothesis of the consciousness, differs from both materialism and conscientialism in this, that it does not conceive of the soul as existing in substance alone nor yet in consciousness alone. On the contrary, both consciousness and body appear to us only as effect of a third thing which comprehends them both, producing the consciousness and also giving form to the raw material. We have already seen that the consciousness must necessarily demand such a profounder 'being,' whereas the materialistic theory demands a formative 'power,' which forms the body and with it the soul. One might call this theory 'monistic,' though it avoids one-sidedness just as it avoids dualism, only that the conception has been overworked, and both the consciential theory and the materialistic theory are—though, after all, incorrectly—described as monistic. We call the theory towards which we are working the *dynamistic* theory, because it represents the nature of the soul as directed force; and we may also call it *vitalistic,* because this force, which gives the body form and engenders the consciousness, proves to be identical with life." [8]

We get a hint of the relation between these three, spirit, soul and body, in the words of *The Secret Doctrine.*

"Life we look upon as the One Form of Existence, manifesting in what is called Matter; or what, incorrectly separating them, we name Spirit, Soul and Matter in man. Matter is the Vehicle for the manifesta-

---
[8] Müller-Freienfels, Richard, *Mysteries of the Soul,* pp. 40, 41, 42.

tion of Soul on this plane of existence, and Soul is the Vehicle on a higher plane for the manifestation of Spirit, and these three are a Trinity synthesized by Life, which pervades them all." [9]

The soul, the self are synonymous terms in Oriental literature. The main treatise upon the Soul, its nature, purpose and mode of existence is that most famous of all the Eastern Scriptures, the *Bhagavad Gita*. Deussen summarises the teaching as to the Atma, the self or soul, as follows:

"If for our present purpose we hold fast to this distinction of the Brahman as the cosmical principle of the universe, the atman as the psychical, the fundamental thought of the entire Upanishad philosophy may be expressed by the simple equation:—

$$Brahman = Atman$$

This is to say—the Brahman, the power which presents itself to us materialized in all existing things, which creates, sustains, preserves, and receives back into itself again all worlds, this eternal infinite divine power is identical with the atman, with that which, after stripping off everything external, we discover in ourselves as our real most essential being, our individual self, the soul. This identity of the Brahman and the atman, of God and the soul, is the fundamental thought of the entire doctrine of the Upanishads. . . .

The atman is, as has often already been pointed out, an idea capable of very different interpretations. The word signifies no more than 'the self,' and the question then arises what we regard as our self. Three positions are here possible, according as by the atman is

---
[9] Blavatsky, H. P., *The Secret Doctrine*, Vol. I, pp. 79, 80.

The Nature of the Soul and Its Location 83

understood (1) the corporeal self, the body; (2) the individual soul, free from the body, which as knowing subject is contrasted with and distinct from the object; or (3) the supreme soul, in which subject and object are no longer distinguished from one another, or which, according to the Indian conception, is the objectless knowing subject." [10]

An Oriental writer comments as follows:

"All organic beings have a principle of self-determination, to which the name of 'soul' is generally given. In the strict sense of the word, 'soul' belongs to every being that has life in it, and the different souls are fundamentally identical in nature. The differences are due to the physical organizations that obscure and thwart the life of the soul. The nature of the bodies in which the souls are incorporated accounts for their various degrees of obscuration.

Each buddhi, with its grasp of senses and the like, is an isolated organism determined by its past karma, and has its own peculiarly associated ignorance (avidya). The ego is the psychological unity of that stream of conscious experiencing which constitutes what we know as the inner life of an empirical self.

The Empirical Self is the mixture of free spirit and mechanism, of purusa and prakriti. . . . Every ego possesses within the gross material body, which suffers dissolution at death, a subtle body, formed of the psychical apparatus, including the senses." [11]

An Indian scripture sums up this teaching as follows:

---
[10] Deussen, Paul, M.D., *The Religion and Philosophy of India*, pp. 39, 94.
[11] Radhakrishnan, S., *Indian Philosophy*, Vol. II, pp. 279, 283, 284, 285.

" 'So there are four Atmas—the life, the mind, the soul, the spirit. The ultimate force which lies at the root of macrocosmic power of the manifestations of soul, mind, and the life-principle, is the spirit'." [12]

All, therefore, appears to be an expression of the life force, and we begin to approach the truth as formulated in the East, that matter is spirit or energy in its lowest manifestation, and spirit is matter in its highest expression. In between these two extremes, and thus manifesting in time and space, come those diversities of the manifested life-consciousness which engross the interest of the religious man, the psychologist, the scientist, and the philosopher, according to their peculiar predilections and tendencies. All are studying the varying aspect of the one animating life.

The differentiations, the terminologies, and the tabulations in connection with these various approaches to truth are the cause of much of the confusion. We are engaged in separating a unified Reality into parts, and in so doing we lose our sense of proportion and over-emphasise that particular part which we happen temporarily to be dissecting. But the whole remains intact, and our realisation of this Reality grows as we become inclusive in our consciousness and participate in a veritable experience.

The testimony to this experience can be traced from the very night of time. From the emergence

---

[12] Prasad, Rama, *Nature's Finer Forces*, p. 121. (Quoted from the Prashnopanishad.)

The Nature of the Soul and Its Location

of the human family in the unfolding evolutionary development of the world plan there has been a paralleling progressive development of the God idea to account for nature and the soul idea to account for man. An anthology of the soul remains as yet to be compiled, the very magnitude of the task probably serving as a deterrent.

Speculation has always been rife as to where the soul was to be found, and where, within the human form, it might be located. A few of the theories propounded might be touched upon here.

Plato held that the vital principle was in the brain and that brain and spinal cord were coördinators of vital force, whilst

Strato placed it in the forepart of the brain, between the eyebrows.

Hippocrates placed the consciousness or soul in the brain and

Herophilus made the calamus scriptorius the chief seat of the soul.

Erasistratos located the soul in the cerebellum, or the little brain, and stated that it was concerned in the coördination of movement.

Galen, the great forerunner of modern medical methods, argued for the fourth ventricle of the brain as the home of the soul in man.

Hippolytus (3rd century A.D.) says: "The membranes in the head are gently moved by the spirit which advances toward the pineal gland. Near this is situated the entrance to the cerebellum which admits the current of spirit and distributes it into the spinal column. This cerebellum by an ineffable and inscrutable process attracts through the pineal gland the spiritual and life giving substance."

St. Augustine regarded the soul as located in the middle ventricle.

The Arabian philosophers, who so strongly moulded thought in the Middle Ages, identified the ventricles of the brain as the seat of the soul or conscious life.

Dr. Hollander tells us that:

"The reason why the ancient philosophers, from whom the Arabs adopted this localization, placed the faculties in certain cells, meaning cavities or ventricles, probably was to give more room for the pneuma, the gaseous substance, to expand.... Some distinguished four regions, as follows: The *first* or anterior ventricle of the brain, which was supposed to look towards the front, was the ventricle of common sense; because from it the nerves of the five outer senses were presumed to branch off, and into it, by the aid of these nerves, all sensations were brought together. The *second* ventricle, connected by a minute opening with the first, was fixed upon as the seat of the imaginative faculty, because the impressions from the five outer senses are transmitted from the first ventricle into it, as a second stage in their progress through the brain. The *third* ventricle was the seat of the understanding; and the *fourth* was sacred to memory, because it was commodiously situated as a storehouse into which the conceptions of the mind, digested in the second ventricle, might be transmitted for attention and accumulation. As a matter of fact, the so-called *anterior* ventricle consists of two ventricles: the right and left lateral ventricles, which communicate with one another and are continuous with the third ventricle—called in ancient times the *middle* ventricle—by the Foramen of Monro; and the third ventricle communicates with the fourth ventricle—called by the ancients the *posterior* ventricle—by the Aqueduct of Sylvius.

The lateral ventricles are roofed over by the corpus callosum; the third is covered by the optic thalamus; and the fourth is situated between cerebellum and pons. ... If the sense of sight and sense of hearing are stimulated at the same time, their effects somehow cohere in conciousness, and the knowledge of this fact inspired the hypothesis of a sensory centre to which the term sensorium commune or common sense was applied. By some this was regarded as the seat of the soul. As parts of the brain are double, the localities to be selected were very limited, and only structures in the middle line could be chosen; as, for example, the pineal gland by Descartes and, as late as the nineteenth century, the optic thalamus by W. B. Carpenter, and the pons cerebri by Herbert Spencer." [13]

Roger Bacon regarded the centre of the brain as the place where the soul could be found.

Ludovico Vives "regarded the soul as the principle, not only of conscious life, but of life in general; the heart is the center of its vital or vegetative activity, the brain of its intellectual activity." [14]

Mundinus, a famous anatomist of the Middle Ages, believed firmly in "animal spirits." He taught that these animal spirits passed into the third ventricle by a narrow passage. He also

---
[13] Hollander, Bernard, M.D., *In Search of the Soul,* Vol. I, p. 97.
[14] Ibid., p. 119.

taught that the cellules of the brain are the seat of the intellect.

Vesalius, the first to discern the difference between the gray and white matter of the brain and to describe the five ventricles, "distinguished three souls . . . and he assigned to the brain the chief soul, the sum of the animal spirits, whose functions were distinctly mental." [15]

Servetus located the soul in the Aqueduct of Sylvius, the channel connecting the third and fourth ventricle of the brain.

Telesio in *De Rerum Natura* "taught that the soul was the subtlest form of matter, a very delicate substance, enclosed within the nervous system and therefore eluding our senses. Its seat is chiefly the brain, but it extends also to the spinal cord, the nerves, arteries, veins, and the covering membranes of the internal organs. . . . Recognizing that the nervous system is in close connection with soul-life, he acknowledged that the soul in man differs only in degree from the soul in animals. He assumed beside the material soul in man, a divine noncorporeal soul directly implanted by God, which united with the material soul." [16]

Willis ascribed the various faculties of the soul, such as mentality, vitality, memory, etc., to different parts of the brain.

Vieussens located the soul in the centrum ovale.

Swedenborg says: "The royal road of the sensa-

---
[15] Hollander, Bernard, M.D., *In Search of the Soul,* Vol. I, p. 129.
[16] Ibid., p. 132.

tions of the body to the soul . . . is through the corpora striata. . . . All determinations of the will also descend by that road. . . . It is the Mercury of Olympus; it announces to the soul what is happening to the body, and it bears the mandates of the soul to the body." [17]

The corpora striata are a pair of large ganglia of the brain immediately under the anterior and superior region of the brain.

Hollis concluded that "both sensation and movement have their power in the medulla of the brain. This therefore is the seat of the soul," and

Charles Bonnet said: "The different senses . . . with which we are endowed . . . have, somewhere, in the brain, secret communications by means of which they may act on one another. The part where the communications take place is that which must be regarded as the seat of the soul. . . . It is by this part that the soul acts on the body, and by the body on so many different beings. Now the soul acts only by the agency of the nerves." [18]

von Sommering localized the seat of the soul in the fluid of the cerebral ventricles, whilst

W. B. Carpenter, the physiologist, regarded the optic thalamus as the seat of the soul life.' [19]

However, from the time of Francis Joseph Gall, the great animist and physician and the founder of the Science of Phrenology, emphasis is no longer

---
[17] Hollander, Bernard, M.D., *In Search of the Soul,* Vol. I, p. 186.
[18] Ibid., p. 190.
[19] The speculations of these various writers have been taken from Dr. Hollander's work quoted above.

laid on the probable location of the soul. The mind has emerged into the limelight; character, ethics and what has been called the Science of Ethology has come into being. The relation of psychical qualities to the brain has become the subject of consideration, and today we have included the glands in our speculation and so carried the idea forward. The modern mechanistic teachings of psychology have temporarily taken the place of the older vitalistic, animistic, and mystical ideas. The materialistic approach, however, has been of profound value. It has brought about two things among many others: It has preserved the balance, first of all, and produced a structure of knowledge, based on natural facts, which has off-set the errors and deductions of the visionary mystic and the superstitions of the religious theologians. Secondly, by means of the conclusions arrived at through the work of the modern psychologists, through the study of the mind, and of its power, and through the influence of such organisations as Christian Science and New Thought, a bridge has been constructed between the East and the West. It is now possible for the Oriental teaching as to the triplicity of soul, mind and brain, to be appreciated and understood. After eliminating certain undesirable features (and there are several) and in collaboration with Western science, light again may stream forth from the East and point the way for humanity into a new state of being, into a fuller realisation of power, and into a truer appreciation of the nature of the human soul. Then perhaps we shall appreciate the truth of Browning's conception of this integrated human being:—

"Three souls which make up one soul; first, to wit,
A soul of each and all the bodily parts,
Seated therein, which works, and is what Does,
And has the use of earth, and ends the man
Downward: but, tending upward for advice,
Grows into, and again is grown into
By the next soul, which, seated in the brain,
Useth the first with its collected use,
And feeleth, thinketh, willeth,—is what Knows:
Which, duly tending upward in its turn,
Grows into, and again is grown into
By the last soul, that uses both the first,
Subsisting whether they assist or no,
And, constituting man's self, is what Is—
And leans upon the former, makes it play,
As that played off the first; and, tending up,
Holds, is upheld by, God, and ends the man
Upward in that dread point of intercourse,
Nor needs a place, for it returns to Him.
What Does, what Knows, what Is; three souls, one man." [20]

---

[20] Browning, Robert, *A Death in the Desert*.

Chapter V

ORIENTAL TEACHING AS TO THE SOUL, ETHER AND ENERGY

"As from its fineness, the all-pervading ether is not touched, so the soul, located in every body, is not touched.

As the one Sun illumines all this world so He that abideth in the body lights up the whole field.

They, who with the eye of Wisdom perceive the distinction between the field and the Knower of the field, and the liberation of being from nature, go to the Supreme." [1]

The literature of the East dealing with the soul and its expression, the etheric or vital body, on the physical plane is immense as a study of the very incomplete bibliography will show. Scattered throughout the Upanishads and the Puranas are thousands of passages dealing with this teaching. Two of the most important sources of information are the *Shiv-Samhita* and the *Shatchakra Nirupanam*.

Sir John Woodroffe (Arthur Avalon) has done much, through his books, to bring a knowledge of this Eastern teaching and of this technique of soul development to the West; he has, through the form in which he has presented it, safeguarded the public also from a too quick comprehension of a most

---
[1] *Bhagavad Gita*, XIII, pp. 32, 33, 34.

Soul, Ether and Energy

dangerous science. A little book by a Hindu physician, well grounded in Western medicine and science, entitled *The Mysterious Kundalini* (Vasant G. Rele) is of real value also.

The danger of this science is well recognised by those who know anything about it. It lies in the fact that through a knowledge of a certain technical method it becomes possible for a man to work actively with the forces of his own nature, as they function through the medium of the vital body. Modern physicians are recognising increasingly the energy factor in connection with man. The electrical nature of the human unit is a natural out-growth of a necessary recognition that the physical body is formed of atoms, as are all forms in the natural world.

The Occidental scientist recognises ether and motion. The Oriental teacher speaks of the akasha and of prana. Both are dealing with the vital livingness which permeates all forms, and is the cause of their coherency, sentiency, and terms of existence. The following passage from the *Kenopanishad* will substantiate this.

"Unmanifested, formless, the one giver of light, is the Great Power; from that appeared the sonoriferous ether (Akasha); from that had birth the tangiferous ether.

From the tangiferous ether, the luminiferous ether, and from this the gustiferous ether; thence was the birth of the odoriferous ether. These are the five ethers and they have five-fold extension.

From these the universe came forth; by these it continues; into these it disappears; among these also it shows itself again." [2]

A resemblance between the luminiferous ether of the ancient Indian scriptures, and the light waves of the modern scientist is obvious. Rama Prasad in an amazingly interesting book called *Nature's Finer Forces* lists four states of subtle matter:

1. Prana or life matter
2. Psychic matter
3. Mental matter
4. Spiritual matter

and it becomes apparent that these four are qualities of the energies which use the Akasha as their medium of expression. A study of the Oriental books gives us a picture of a material world which is brought into being and animated by a subjective world of forces, which use the ether (Akasha) as their playground, and are responsible for all forms, qualities and differentiations in the phenomenal world.

The following extracts from *The Serpent Power* give the Oriental teaching about matter and ether.

"Recent scientific research has shown that this original substance cannot be scientific 'matter'—that is, that which has mass, weight, and inertia. Matter has been dematerialised and reduced, according to current hy-

---
[2] Kenopanishad—Quoted by Rama Prasad in *Nature's Finer Forces*, pp. 187-188.

potheses, to something which differs profoundly from 'matter' as known by the senses. This ultimate substance is stated to be Ether in a state of motion. The present scientific hypothesis would appear to be as follows. There is no such thing as scientific 'Matter.' If there seems to be such, this is due to the action of Shakti as Maya. The ultimate and simplest physical factor from which the universe has arisen is motion of and in a substance, called 'ether,' which is not scientific 'matter.' The motions of this substance give rise from the realistic point of view to the notion of 'matter.' Matter is thus at base one, notwithstanding the diversity of its forms. Its ultimate element is on the final analysis of one kind, and the differences in the various kinds of matter depend on the various movements of the ultimate particle and its succeeding combinations. Given such unity of base, it is possible that one form of matter may pass into another." [3]

In another book Arthur Avalon says:

"In the first place, it is now admitted that 'matter,' even with the addition of all possible forces, is insufficient to explain many phenomena, such as those of light; and it has, accordingly, come to be an article of scientific faith that there is a substance called 'Ether'; a medium which, filling the universe, transports by its vibrations the radiations of light, heat, electricity, and perhaps action from a distance, such as the attraction exercised between heavenly bodies. It is said, however, that this Ether is not 'matter,' but differs profoundly from it, and that it is only our infirmity of knowledge which obliges us, in our attempted description of it, to borrow comparisons from 'matter' in its ordinary physical sense, which alone is known by our senses. But if we assume the existence of Ether, we know that

---
[3] Avalon, Arthur (Sir John Woodroffe), *The Serpent Power*, p. 89.

'material' bodies immersed in it can change their places therein. In fact, to use an Indian expression, the characteristic property of the vibrations of the Akasha Tattva is to make the space in which the other Tattvas and their derivatives exist. With 'Matter' and Ether as its materials, Western purely 'scientific' theories have sought to construct the world." [4]

"Many people were wont, as some still are, to laugh at the idea of Maya. Was not matter solid, permanent and real enough? But according to science what are we (as physical beings) at base? The answer is, infinitely tenuous formless energy which materialises into relatively stable, yet essentially transitory, forms. . . . The process by which the subtle becomes gradually more and more gross continues until it develops into what a friend of mine calls the 'crust' of solid matter (Parthivabhuta). This whilst it lasts is tangible enough. But it will not last for ever and in some radioactive substances dissociates before our eyes." [5]

Vivekananda, who did so much to reveal the soul of India to the West, says:

"According to the philosophers of India, the whole universe is composed of two materials, one of which they call *Akasa*. It is the omnipresent all penetrating existence. Everything that has form, everything that is the result of the compounds, is evolved out of this *Akasa*. It is the *Akasa* that becomes the air, that becomes the liquids, that becomes the solids; it is the *Akasa* that becomes the sun, the earth, the moon, the stars, the comets; it is the *Akasa* that becomes the body, the animal body, the planets, every form that we see, everything that can be sensed, everything that exists. It itself cannot be perceived; it is so subtle that

---

[4] Woodroffe, Sir John (Arthur Avalon), *Shakti and Shakta*, p. 167.
[5] Woodroffe, Sir John (Arthur Avalon), *Shakti and Shakta*, p. 170.

it is beyond all ordinary perception; it can only be seen when it has become gross, has taken form. At the beginning of creation there is only this *Akasa*; at the end of the cycle the solids, the liquids, and the gases all melt into the *Akasa* again, and the next creation similarly proceeds out of this *Akasa*.

By what power is this *Akasa* manufactured into this universe? By the power of *Prana*. Just as *Akasa* is the infinite omnipresent material of this universe, so is this *Prana* the infinite omnipresent manifesting power of this universe. At the beginning and at the end of a cycle everything becomes *Akasa,* and all the forces that are in the universe resolve back into the *Prana*; in the next cycle, out of this *Prana,* is evolved everything that we call energy, everything that we call force. It is the *Prana* that is manifesting as motion; it is the *Prana* that is manifesting as gravitation, as magnetism. It is the *Prana* that is manifesting as the actions of the body, as the nerve currents, as thought force. From thought, down to the lowest physical force, everything is but the manifestation of *Prana*. The sum-total of all force in the universe, mental or physical, when resolved back to its original state, is called *Prana*...." [6]

A more modern writer, Ramacharaka, says:

"In order to avoid misconceptions arising from the various theories regarding this great principle, which theories are usually attached to some name given the principle, we, in this work, will speak of the principle as '*Prana,*' this word being the Sanscrit term meaning 'Absolute Energy.' Many occult authorities teach that the principle which the Hindus term '*Prana*' is the universal principle of energy or force, and that all energy or force is derived from that principle, or, rather,

---

[6] Vivekananda, Swami, *Raja Yoga*, pp. 29, 30.

is a particular form of manifestation of that principle. ... We may consider it as the active principle of life—Vital Force, if you please. It is found in all forms of life, from the amoeba to man—from the most elementary form of plant life to the highest form of animal life. *'Prana'* is all pervading. It is found in all things having life, and as the occult philosophy teaches that life is in all things—in every Atom—the apparent lifelessness of some things being only a lesser degree of manifestation, we may understand their teachings that *'Prana'* is everywhere, in everything. *'Prana'* must not be confounded with the Ego—that bit of Divine Spirit in every soul, around which clusters matter and energy. *'Prana'* is merely a form of energy used by the Ego in its material manifestation. When the Ego leaves the body, the *'Prana,'* being no longer under its control, responds only to the order of the individual atoms, or groups of atoms, forming the body, and as the body disintegrates and is resolved to its original elements, each atom takes with it sufficient *'Prana'* to enable it to form new combinations, the unused *'Prana'* returning to the great universal storehouse from which it came. With the Ego in control, cohesion exists and the atoms are held together by the Will of the Ego.

"*'Prana'* is the name by which we designate a universal principle, which principle is the essence of all motion, force or energy, whether manifested in gravitation, electricity, the revolution of the planets, and all forms of life, from the highest to the lowest. It may be called the soul of Force and Energy in all their forms, and that principle which, operating in a certain way, causes that form of activity which accompanies life." [7]

This prana is therefore the universal life principle in all forms, and the so-called energies or

---

[7] Ramacharaka, Yogi, *The Hindu-Yogi Science of Breath*, pp. 16, 17.

life of the human body are the differentiated quota of that universal principle which any particular human soul has appropriated.

The energies which utilise the akasha (ether) in the universe are divided into three main divisions according to the Ageless Wisdom.

1. *Fohat,* is analogous to what the Christian regards as the spirit; it is the will-to-exist, the determining life principle of God, Who, we can predicate, is the sum total of all forms, and of all states of consciousness; it is divine Purpose, actively functioning.

2. *Prana,* is analogous to the activity of the consciousness principle, the Soul of the Christian. This prana is an effect of the union of spirit or life, and matter or substance, and demonstrates as the energy of the form, as it produces cohesion, animation and sensitivity, carrying out divine purpose.

3. *Kundalini,* as it is called in connection with the human form, is the force latent in matter itself; it is the integral life of the atom, apart from any form in which that atom may participate in its tiny cycle of experience.

Shakti is power or energy. Arthur Avalon defines it as follows:

"What then is Shakti and how does it come about that there is some principle of unconsciousness in things; a fact which cannot be denied. Shakti comes from the root 'shak' 'to be able,' 'to have power.' It may be applied to any form of activity. The power to burn is Shakti of fire and so forth. These are all forms of activity which are ultimately reducible to the Primordial Shakti (Adya Shakti) whence every other form of Power proceeds."[8]

These three types of energy are therefore aspects of the one universal life, as it expresses itself through a solar system, utilising the ether as its medium or field of activity, and producing therefrom all the objective forms. The process repeats itself in man, according to the Hindu philosophy.

The physical body is the expression in its component parts or atoms of the third type of energy, and the sum-total of that atomic energy is called Kundalini:

"The centre where all residual sensations are, as it were, stored up is called Mul-adhara chakra, and the coiled up energy of action is Kundalini, 'the coiled up'."
It is the individual bodily representative of the great cosmic power (Shakti) which created and sustains the universe."[9]

The physical body itself is often regarded as an atom in the body of the human kingdom, and in this case the Kundalini energy, localised as it is supposed to be in a centre at the base of the spine, would be a positive nucleus, with the other atoms of the body regarded as electronic in nature.

The vital body, or body of ether, is the medium

---
[8] Woodroffe, Sir John (Arthur Avalon), *Shakti and Shakta*, p. 207.
[9] Rele, Vasant G., *The Mysterious Kundalini*, p. 40.

Soul, Ether and Energy

for the expression of the life soul, that sentient vivifying duality which we call *prana*. This dual energy has two positive centres in the vital body and consequently in the physical—one in the heart, where feeling and sentiency are claimed to be centred, and another in the head where the mind and the spiritual consciousness find expression.

Dr. Rele says that "Prana proper is located between the larynx and the base of the heart."

"The heart more than the head occupies the attention of the thinkers of the Upanishads. It is there that the vital breaths reside. Not only the five pranas, but also eye, ear, speech, and manas originate from the heart. The heart and not the head is the home of manas; and the former therefore is the centre also of conscious life. In sleep the organs of the soul remain in the heart, and there also they gather at death; 'through the heart we recognize forms,' through the heart we recognize faith, beget children, know the truth, on it speech also is based, while the further question on what the heart is based is angrily rejected. Not the organs however alone, but all beings are based upon and supported by the heart; and even setting aside the actual definition of the heart as Brahman, it is yet the empirical home of the soul, and therefore of Brahman:—'here within the heart is a cavity, wherein he resides, the lord of the universe, the ruler of the universe, the chief of the universe.' The heart is called *hridayam*, because 'it is he' who dwells 'in the heart' (hridi ayam, Chand. 8.3.3.), small as a grain of rice or barley; an inch in height the purusha dwells in the midst of the body, as the self of created things in the heart." [10]

---
[10] Deussen, Dr. Paul, *The Philosophy of the Upanishads*, pp. 286, 287.

"Similarly numerous passages in the later Upanishads celebrate Brahman as 'implanted in the cavity of the heart.' The identity of the atman in us with the atman of the universe is expressed by the *tat tvam asi* of Chand. 6.8-16, and also by the *etad vai tad*, 'in truth this is that,' of Brih. 5.4, which is probably an imitation of the other. The same formula is found twelve times in Kath. 4. 3-6. 1, in a prose passage appended to the verses. The highest bliss, according to Kath. 5. 14, consists in the consciousness of this thought. We quote in this connection only Kath. 4.12-13:—

> An inch in height, here in the body
> The purusha dwells,
> Lord of the past and the future;
> He who knows him frets no more,—
>   In truth, this is that.
>
> Like flame without smoke, an inch in height
> The purusha is in size,
> Lord of the past and the future;
> It is he to-day and also to-morrow,—
>   In truth, this is that.[11]

As here the purusha is compared to a smokeless flame, so in imitation of this passage, in S'vet. 6. 19, it is likened to a fire whose fuel is consumed; while in S'vet. 5. 9, the contrast between the atman within us and the atman in the universe is pushed to an extreme:—

> Split a hundred times the tip of a hair,
> And take a hundredth part thereof;
> That I judge to be the size of the soul,
> Yet it goes to immortality.

---
[11] Deussen, Dr. Paul, *Philosophy of the Upanishads*, p. 170.

Soul, Ether and Energy

The description of the atman as a smokeless flame in the heart has been developed in the Yogi Upanishads into the picture of the tongue of flame in the heart, the earliest occurrence of which is perhaps Mahan. 11. 6-12." [12]

The Scriptures are full of references to the fact that Atman, the self, is found in the heart, from whence it expresses itself as the *life principle through the medium of the blood*. *The soul nature, or the rational mind and the self-conscious individual expresses itself in the head* and from that position governs the nervous system:

"It has now been proved, that the highest centres are located in the cortex of the brain, where knowledge of action and sensation is manifested. These centres are both receiving i.e. sensory; and directing i.e. motor, and have their subsidiary centres in the two large swellings called the basal-ganglia in each hemisphere of the brain. They are known as thalamus and corpus striatum. The first one is auxiliary to the chief sensory centre and the second one auxiliary to the chief motor centre in the cortex of the brain. Normally, the auxiliary motor centres are more or less under the control of the will. . . . The Yogi is concerned with the subsidiary nerve centres in the thalamus. The normal function of the thalamus is to receive sensations from all parts of the body, which are relayed to it through the spinal cord, before they reach the chief centre.

As this is the highest reflex centre in the brain and as all impressions ascend to it, it is called the Udana-prana. The last relay in the cord, from which it receives impulses, is from that portion of the cord,

---
[12] Deussen, Dr. Paul, *Philosophy of the Upanishads*, p. 171.

called the Bulb, which is on a level with the root of the nose. Udana-prana is, therefore, said to rule the portion of the head above this point.

The Yogi, by a conscious control over the Udana-prana, suppresses all incoming and outgoing sensations into it, and this is necessary to prevent the distraction of the mind which he is anxious to control." [13]

Srinivasa Iyengar makes the following postulates and states that all the schools of thought, except the school of crude Nihilism accept them.

1. Man is a complex of consciousness, mind and body.

2. The Atma (self) is of the nature of the consciousness and is immutable.

3. Mind, though an inner organ, is material, and is other than the atman.

4. All energy in the universe is personal, *i.e.,* bound up with consciousness.

5. This energy is prana, which is intermediate between mind and matter.

"Hindu philosophy regards Prana and not motion as the fundamental energy of the cosmos. Prana is conceived as a power coming from or started by the Purusha (Spirit aspect—A.A.B.) and acting on matter."

"All the energy of animals is nervous energy till it leaves the muscles and acts on outside objects. This nervous energy is called Prana. Western Science has for a hundred years unsuccessfully tried to explain nervous energy as a form of mechanical motion; Eastern Philosophy reverses the process and derives me-

---
[13] Rele, Vasant G., *The Mysterious Kundalini,* p. 70.

Soul, Ether and Energy

chanical motion from Prana, or energy accompanied by consciousness.

Prana corresponds to the Psychikon pneuma, animal spirits, of Greek philosophy, a category which is intermediate between spirit and matter, and brings them into relation with each other." [14]

Arthur Avalon says:

"Various people have in antiquity assigned to various parts of the body the 'seat of the soul' or life, such as the blood, the heart, and the breath. Generally the brain was not so regarded. The Vaidik system posits the heart as the chief centre of Consciousness—a relic of which notion we also still preserve in such phrases as 'take it to heart' and to 'learn by heart.' Sadhaka, which is one of the five functions of Pitta, and which is situated in the heart, indirectly assists in the performance of cognitive functions by keeping up the rhythmic cardiac contractions, and it has been suggested that it was perhaps this view of the heart's construction which predisposed Indian physiologists to hold it to be the seat of cognition. According to the Tantras, however, the chief centers of consciousness are to be found in the Chakras of the cerebro-spinal system and in the upper brain (Sahasrara), which they describe, though the heart is also recognized as a seat of the Jivatma, or embodied spirit, in its aspect as Prana." [15]

These two points of view account probably for the phenomenon of the human being. As evolution proceeds it may be found and demonstrated that the positive centre or nucleus for the life of

---
[14] Iyengar, P. T. Srinivasa, *Outlines of Indian Philosophy*, pp. 58. 59.
[15] Avalon, Arthur (Sir John Woodroffe), *The Serpent Power*, p. 3.

the material form is located at the base of the spine, that the positive centre for the life of the sentient conscious man is in the heart, whilst the positive centre for the mind and the spiritual life principles is in the head.

The whole scheme and technique of the Oriental teaching as to the centres in man have in view the increasing display of prana or life-soul energy. Through an understanding of this a man can demonstrate (through the automaton of the physical body) those soul powers and spiritual qualities which are the inheritance of the spiritual man, the Soul.

The object, therefore, of all methods and practices is to bring about conscious union with the soul, and produce the subordination of the two lower energies, those of matter and those of the sentient mental nature, to the highest of the three energies, the spiritual life. When this is accomplished, the spiritual life principle animates a soul which knows no barriers and limitations because it has brought its mechanism to the highest state of perfection. Matter has been raised into heaven, and hence the Hindu teaching that the Kundalini fire, the energy of matter (sometimes called the mother) has eventually to be raised from its position at the base of the spine up into the head. This is a correspondence to the Roman Catholic teaching as to the Assumption of the Virgin-Mother into Heaven to take her place by the side of her Son, the Christ, the Soul. This has to be brought about consciously by the soul or self, seated in the mind and brain consciousness, and from there assuming control of the energies of the entire natural man. This is Yoga or union, which is not only a mystical experience, but a vital or physical one also. This is the at-one-ment of the Christian. It is an integration of the entire man, physical, sentient, and mental, and then a conscious unification with the universal soul. Dr. Rele says:

"The word 'Yoga' is derived from the root 'Yuga' to join or to weld together. Just as in welding, two pieces of the same metal are made to become one by the process of heating and hammering, so also in the Yoga of Indian Philosophy, the embodied spirit 'Jivatma,' which is a part of the universal spirit 'Paramatma,' is made to become one with the Universal Spirit by certain physical and mental exercises.

Yoga is the science which raises the capacity of the human mind to respond to higher vibrations, and to perceive, catch, and assimilate the infinite conscious movements going on around us in the universe." [16]

René Guénon sums up the result of this union in the following terms:

"Deliverance or Union, which is one and the same thing, involves, as we have already stated, 'over and above,' the possession of all states, since it is the perfect realization (*sadhana*) and totalization of the being; it is moreover of little import whether these states are or are not actually manifested, since it is only as permanent and immutable possibilities that they are to be metaphysically considered. 'Lord of many states by

---

[16] Rele, Vasant G., *The Mysterious Kundalini*, pp. 13, 14.

the simple effect of his will, the Yogi only concerns himself with one, leaving the others void of the animating breath (*prana*), as so many unused instruments, he can animate more than one form in the same way that a single lamp may supply more than one wick.' 'The *Yogi*,' says Aniruddha, 'is in direct connexion with the primordial principle of the Universe, and in consequence (secondarily) with the whole of space, of time and of things,' that is to say, with manifestation, and, more particularly, with the human state in all its modifications." [17]

---

[17] Guénon, René, *Man and His Becoming*, p. 238.

Chapter VI

SEVEN CENTRES OF FORCE

In the previous chapter we have seen that, according to the Eastern teaching, the vital or etheric body is constituted of ether and acts as the conductor of prana which is the life principle and energises matter and produces form. The vital body also embodies that sentient principle in nature called the soul, or rather the vital body is the expression and vehicle of the soul.

The main characteristic of the soul is consciousness. The soul as life is "seated in the heart," and as rational spiritual consciousness is "seated on the throne between the eyebrows." René Guénon expresses this as follows:

"Thus, what dwells in the vital centre, from the physical point of view, is ether; from the psychic point of view, it is the 'living soul,' and so far we are not transcending the realm of individual possibilities; but also, and above all, from the metaphysical point of view, it is the principal and unconditioned 'Self.' It is, therefore, truly the 'Universal Spirit' (*Atma*), which is, in reality, *Brahma* Itself, the 'Supreme Ruler'; and thus the designation of this center as *Brahma-pura* is found to be fully justified. But *Brahma,* considered in this manner as within man (and one might consider it in like manner in relation to every state of being) is called *Purusha,* because It rests or dwells in the individuality ... as in a town (*puri-shaya*) for *pura*, in its proper and literal sense, signifies town'." [1]

The life force has seven main points of contact with the physical body, called the seven centres.

These seven force centres transmit the life force, and are the agents of the soul. They maintain bodily existence and produce its activity.

The Dreamer in his book, says:

"What then are the centres of man? They are the reflections in the respective nuclei of the upadhi of the one Self. If we study the workings of the impregnation of matter by Divine Energy, sometimes spoken of as the life waves, we shall see how, from the projection of the Self into the limits of objectivity called matter, certain qualities are imparted to matter developing into what are called tattvas. Each tattva has got for its ensouled life a tanmatra, or a modification of the Divine consciousness. In each tattva, therefore, we have the Divine consciousness as the central life, while the idea of resistance forms the outer wall."

"We have seen that the Self, in virtue of its power of manifestation, reflects itself in the various upadhis, developing in them artificial centres which form, so to say, at one and the same time the nucleus of the upadhis as well as the representatives of the Self in the respective planes." [2]

The Indian name of a force centre is "chakra." The location of the seven centres of force (with their complete Indian names) are as follows, from the head downwards:

---

[1] Guénon, René, *Man and His Becoming*, pp. 44, 45.
[2] Dreamer, The, *Studies in the Bhagavad Gita*, pp. 37, 40, 107.

The Seven Centres of Force

1. Head centre — sahasrara chakra
2. Centre between eyebrows — ajna chakra
3. Throat centre — vishuddha chakra
4. Heart or cardiac centre — anahata chakra
5. Solar plexus centre — manipura chakra
6. Sacral or sexual centre — svadhisthana chakra
7. Centre at base of spine — muladhara chakra

It will be noted that there are four centres above the diaphragm and three below.

Much has been written and more could be said, about these force centres or chakras, but the following will serve as an introductory summary.

The force centres carry pranic energy for every part of the body and are in close relation to the nervous system in its three divisions, namely: the cerebro-spinal, sympathetic and peripheral.

From the force centres the vital or pranic energy is distributed along subtle lines of direction. These lines are called "nadis" and are closely related to the nerves and at the same time to the arteries; they apparently underlie the corporeal nervous system. In *Man and His Becoming* we read:

"As regards the nadis or arteries of the subtle form, they must not be confounded with the corporeal arteries through which the circulation of the blood is effected, and, physiologically, they correspond rather to the ramifications of the nervous system, for they are expressly described as luminous; but as fire is in some sort polarized into heat and light, the subtle state is linked to the corporeal state in two different and complementary ways, by the blood as to the caloric quality, and by the nervous system as to the luminous quality. However, it must be clearly understood that, between the *nadis* and the nerves, there is still only a simple correspondence and not an identification, since the former are not corporeal, and that we are dealing in reality with two different realms in the integral individuality. Similarly, when a relation is affirmed between the function of these *nadis* and respiration, because this is essential to the maintenance of life and corresponds truly with the principal vital activity, it must by no means be concluded on this account that they can be conceived as a kind of channel in which the air circulates; this would be to confuse the 'vital breath' (*prana*), which properly belongs to the subtle manifestation, with a corporeal element.

It is stated that the total number of *nadis* is seventy-two thousand; according to other texts, however, it should be seven hundred and twenty millions; but the difference here is more apparent than real, since, as always holds good in such cases, these numbers must be taken symbolically, not literally." [3]

Rama Prasad, who uses the Indian word lotus for chakra or force centre, makes an interesting comment in this connection:

"The nervous plexuses of the modern anatomists coincide with these centres. From what has been said above it will appear that the centres are constituted by bloodvessels. But the only difference between the nerves and the bloodvessels is the difference between

---
[3] Guénon, René, *Man and His Becoming*, pp. 136, 137.

The Seven Centres of Force

the vehicles of the positive and negative Pranas. The nerves are the positive, the bloodvessels the negative system of the body. Wherever there are nerves there are correponding bloodvessels. Both of them are indiscriminately called Nadis. One set has for its centre the lotus of the Heart, the other the thousand-petalled lotus of the brain. The system of bloodvessels is an exact picture of the nervous system, is, in fact, only its shadow. Like the heart, the brain has its upper and lower divisions—the cerebrum and the cerebellum—and, as well, its right and left divisions." [4]

The force centres are situated up the spinal column and in the head. Arthur Avalon says:

"A description of the Chakras involves, in the first place, an account of the Western anatomy and physiology of the central and sympathetic nervous systems; secondly, an account of the Tantrik nervous system and Chakras; and, lastly, the correlation, so far as that is possible, of the two systems on the anatomical and physiological side, for the rest is in general peculiar to Tantrik Occultism.

The Tantrik theory regarding the Chakras and Sahasrara is concerned on the physiological side ... with the central spinal system, comprising the brain or encephalon, contained within the skull, and the spinal cord, contained within the vertebral column (Merudanda). It is to be noted that, just as there are five centres (Chakras) hereinafter described, the vertebral column itself is divided into five regions, which, commencing from the lowest, are the coccygeal, consisting of four imperfect vertebræ, often united together into one bone called the coccyx; the sacral region, consisting of five vertebræ united together to form a single

---
[4] Prasad, Rama, *Nature's Finer Forces*, pp. 45-46.

bone, the sacrum; the lumbar region, or region of the loins, consisting of five vertebræ; the dorsal region, or region of the back, consisting of twelve vertebræ; and the cervical region, or region of the neck, consisting of seven vertebræ. As exhibited by segments, the cord shows different characteristics in different regions. Roughly speaking these correspond to the regions which are assigned to the governing control of the Muladhara, Svadhishthana, Manipura, Anahata, and Vishuddha centres, or Chakras.[5] The central system has relation with the periphery through the thirty-one spinal and twelve cranial nerves, which are both afferent and efferent or sensory and motor, arousing sensation or stimulating action. Of the cranial nerves, the last six arise from the spinal bulb (medulla), and the other six, except the olfactory and optic nerves, from the parts of the brain just in front of the bulb. Writers of the Yoga and Tantra schools use the term Nadi, by preference, for nerves. They also, it has been said, mean cranial nerves when they speak of Shiras, never using the latter for arteries, as is done in the medical literature. It must, however, be noted that the Yoga Nadis are not the ordinary material nerves, but subtler lines of direction along which the vital forces go. The spinal nerves, after their exit from the inter-vertebral foramina, enter into communication with the gangliated cords of the sympathetic nervous system which lie on each side of the vertebral column. The spinal cord extends in the case of man from the upper border of the atlas, below the cerebellum, passing into the medulla, and finally opening into the fourth ventricle of the brain, and descends to the second lumbar vertebra, where it tapers to a point, called the filum terminale."[6]

---

[5] These regions are the base of the spine, sacral center, solar plexus center, heart center and throat center.
[6] Avalon, Arthur, *The Serpent Power*, pp. 123-125.

The Seven Centres of Force

As the foregoing quotation refers to the Tantrik system, it should be noted that reference is made to an Indian system of energy control safe only for those of the highest moral character and purity of life and thought. Certain degraded practices and schools, occurring both in the East and the West, teaching so-called Tantrik practices cannot be too severely condemned.

These force centres are not merely situated up the spinal column and in the head as we have just shown, but they are related to one another through the medium of the spinal column—a relationship too intricate to be detailed here.

Of the seven centres, two are in the head and five in the spinal column. The two centres in the head have a direct relation to the faculties of mind and motion. The sahasrara centre (head centre) called usually the thousand-petalled lotus, is the embodiment of spiritual energy, demonstrating as Will, as the abstract or spiritual mind, and as the intuition. The ajna centre, or the centre between the eyebrows, concerns the lower mind and psychic nature of that integrated organism we call man, the personality.

The five centres in the spinal column concern the varying activities of the organism as the man demonstrates his animal instinct, his emotional reactions and his life intention. They are largely directed by the force pouring into and issuing from the head centres.

In *The Serpent Power* it is stated that:

"The centres influence not only the muscular combinations concerned in volitional movements, but also the functions of vascular innervation, secretion, and the like, which have their proximate centres in the spinal cord. The cerebral centres are said, however, to control these functions only in relation with the manifestations of volition, feeling, and emotion; whereas the spinal centres with the subordinate sympathetic system are said to constitute the mechanism of unconscious adaptation, in accordance with the varying conditions of stimuli which are essential to the continued existence of the organism. The Medulla, again, is also both a path of communication between the higher centres and the periphery and an independent centre regulating functions of the greatest importance in the system. It is to be noted that the nerve fibres which carry motor impulses descending from the brain to the spinal cord cross over rather suddenly from one side to the other on their way through the spinal bulb (medulla), a fact which has been noted in the Tantras in the description of the Mukta Triveni. The latter is connected by numerous afferent and efferent tracts with the cerebellum and cerebral ganglia. Above the cerebellum is the cerebrum, the activity of which is ordinarily associated with conscious volition and ideation and the origination of voluntary movements. The notion of Consciousness, which is the introspective subject-matter of psychology, must not, however, be confused with that of physiological function. There is therefore no organ of consciousness, simply because 'Consciousness' is not an organic conception, and has nothing to do with the physiological conception of energy, whose inner introspective side it presents. Consciousness in itself is the Atma. Both mind and body, of which latter the brain is a part, are imperfect or veiled expressions of Consciousness, which in the case of body is so veiled that it has the appearance of unconsciousness. The living brain is constituted of gross sensible matter (Mahabhuta) infused by Prana. Its material has been worked up so as to constitute a suitable vehicle for the expression of consciousness in the form of mind (Antahkarana). As consciousness is not a property of the body, neither is it a mere function of the brain. The fact that mental consciousness is affected or disappears with disorder of the brain proves the necessity of the latter for the expression of *such* consciousness, and not that consciousness is inherent alone in brain or that it is the property of the same. On each side of the vertebral column there is a chain of ganglia connected with nerve fibre, called the sympathetic cord (Ida and Pingala), extending all the way from the base of the skull to the coccyx. This is in communication with the spinal cord. It is noteworthy that there is in the thoracic and lumbar regions a ganglion of each chain corresponding with great regularity to each spinal nerve, though in the cervical region many of them appear to be missing; and that extra large clusters of nervous structure are to be found in the region of the heart, stomach, and lungs, the regions governed by the Anahata, Manipura, and Vishuddha, respectively, the three upper of the five Chakras hereinafter described. From the sympathetic chain on each side nerve fibres pass to the viscera of the abdomen and thorax. From these, nerves are also given off which pass back into the spinal nerves, and others which pass into some of the cranial nerves; these are thus distributed to the blood vessels of the limbs, trunk, and other parts to which the spinal or cranial nerves go. The sympathetic nerves chiefly carry impulses which govern the muscular tissue of the viscera and the muscular coat of the small arteries of the various tissues. It is through the sympathetic that the tone of the bloodvessels is kept up by the action of the vaso-motor centre in the spinal bulb. The sympathetic, however, derives the impulses which it distributes from the central nervous system; these do not arise in the sympathetic self. The impulses issue from the spinal cord by the anterior roots of the spinal nerves, and pass through short branches into the sympathetic chains. The work of the sympathetic systems controls and influences the circulation, digestion, and respiration.

The anatomical arrangement of the central nervous system is excessively intricate, and the events which take place in that tangle of fibre, cell and fibril, are, on the other hand, even now almost unknown. And so it has been admitted that in the description of the physiology of the central nervous system we can as yet do little more than trace the paths by which impulses *may* pass between one portion of the system and another, and from the anatomical connections deduce, with more or less probability, the nature of the physiological nexus which its parts form with each other and the rest of the body. In a general way, however, there may (it is said) be reasons to suppose that there ar nervous centres in the central system related in special way to special mechanisms, sensory, secretory, or motor, and that centres, such as the alleged genito-spinal centre, for a given physiological action exist in a definite portion of the spinal cord. It is the subtle aspect of such centres as expressions of consciousness (Chaitanya) embodied in various forms of Maya Shakti which is here called Chakra. These are related through intermediate conductors with the gross organs of generation, micturition, digestion, cardiac action, and respiration in ultimate relation with the Muladhara, Svadhishthana, Manipura, Anahata, and Vishuddha Chakras respectively, just as tracts have been assigned in special, even if not exclusive, relation with

The Seven Centres of Force 119

various perceptive, volitional, and ideative processes." [7]

These centres vary in activity according to the evolutionary status of the individual. In some people certain centres are "awake" and in others the same centres may be relatively quiescent. In certain types, the solar plexus centre will be active or dominant, in others the heart, in still others the throat. In very few as yet, is the head centre active. Speaking largely, in savage people and the little evolved, the three centres below the diaphragm— the centre at the base of the spine, the sacral centre and the solar plexus centre—are alive and dominant, but the centres above the diaphragm are "asleep." In average humanity the throat centre is beginning to make itself felt with the head and heart centres still asleep. In the highly evolved human being, the race leader, the intuitive philosopher and the scientist, and in the great saints, both the head and heart centres are making their vibrations felt, priority between head and heart being determined by type, and the quality of the emotional and mental consciousness.

According, then, to the development of the man these force centres become alive and dominant, and according to their aliveness various types of activity make their presence felt. The centres below the diaphragm govern the physical life of the material form and the animal psychic life, found both

---
[7] Avalon, Arthur, *The Serpent Power*, pp. 126-129.

in man and in the animal. Those above the diaphragm concern the intellectual and spiritual life and bring about those activities in which man demonstrates that his status is different to, and higher than that of the animal, and that he is climbing upward on the ladder of evolution.

Such in brief is the teaching of the East with regard to the seven centres of force or chakras.

When we compare the Eastern Doctrine of the seven centres with the Western doctrine of glands, we find first of all a striking fact with regard to locality. The seven centres of force are to be found in the same region where the glands are located, and each centre of force might well be (and according to Indian teaching is) the source of power and of life for the corresponding gland. The following comparative table shows this identity of location.

CENTRES	GLANDS
Head centre	Pineal gland
Centre between eyebrows	Pituitary body
Throat centre	Thyroid gland
Heart centre	Thymus gland
Solar plexus centre	Pancreas
Sacral centre	The gonads
Centre at base of spine	Adrenal glands

A second fact, even more striking than the first, is that the force centres which are awake conform to the glands whose functions are known and of

The Seven Centres of Force

which most of the secretions or hormones, have been discovered. The centres that are asleep or awakening in advanced members of the race, conform to the glands whose functions are relatively unknown and whose secretions in the main have not been isolated. It will be noted for example that Dr. Berman states that the secretion of the pineal gland, one of the two in the pituitary body and the thymus gland, are listed as unknown, as is the secretion of the cortex adrenal gland. These conform to the sleeping or awakening heart centre, throat centre, centre in the head, and at the base of the spine.

Is this an interesting coincidence? Or are we faced with the fact that in each case these glands with the undiscovered hormones, are allied to a centre which is asleep, not yet awakened in average humanity?

I believe it will eventually be established that the glands have been brought into being through the energy of the centres, for those centres which, in average humanity, are awake and functioning seem to be related to glands, whose peculiar secretion has been isolated, and its action in relation to the bloodstream known, whilst those centres which are as yet asleep and undeveloped seem to be allied to glands whose secretion is only partially known or totally unknown. It is in any case worthy of consideration.

The Occidental psychologists are consequently right when they state that a man is what his glands make him, and that we are no better or worse than our peculiar endocrine system. But the reason for this may lie in the correctness of the Oriental theory as to the force centres. The condition of the glands and their super-activity or sub-normality, and their right or wrong functioning may be determined by the state of those centres. The glands are only outer symbols, the visible, material aspect of a far greater and more intricate system. They are determined by the character of the soul life which plays through them, and the soul which controls and dominates all.

The state of the centres, then, is dependent upon the type and quality of soul force vibrating through them. In the undeveloped person it is simply the life force, prana, which is active and registers. This nurtures the animal life and brings the lower centres (the centre at the base of the spine and the sacral centre) into activity. Later, as man develops, the consciousness, soul-aspect, gradually makes its presence felt and brings the solar plexus centre into activity. This centre is the seat of the lower psychic sentient life both in man and in the animal, and is often referred to as the instinctual brain. Bhagavan Das teaches us that:

"It is worth noting that in Sanskrit literature the navel is often treated as more central and almost more essential to the organism than the heart. Indications of the importance of the heart are not wanting, it is true, . . . but it is probable that physiologically the 'navel' was the more vital organ in the earlier stages

The Seven Centres of Force

of evolution, and is even at the present stage more essentially connected with desire proper than the heart which may perhaps be regarded as connected with the actional sub-division of desire." [8]

He quotes Mrs. Besant also in the following paragraph:

"The 'navel' represents the solar plexus, perhaps the most important plexus of the sympathetic system; it controls the digestive tract, and sends its branches to liver, spleen, stomach, as well as to the alimentary canal and generative organs. Nor is it unconnected with the lungs and heart. It may be regarded as the brain of the sympathetic system, and responds with dangerous facility to thought; concentration on it, often rashly undertaken, is apt to result in a peculiarly intractable form of nervous disease. Emotions set up in it violent disturbances, and the feeling of a nausea, which often follows an emotional shock, is due to its excited action." [9]

Man functions today through the medium of these three centres for the most part. The forces of the body serve to feed and stimulate the sex life through the gonads, they create the urge to combat and to evolve through the adrenal glands, the glands of combat, and of struggle; they govern the psychic instinctual life through the solar plexus. Thus the personal man is mobilised and becomes a conscious sentient human being. As his evolution proceeds, the self or soul becomes more and more

---
[8] Das, Bhagavan, *The Science of the Sacred Word*, Vol. I, p. 82, footnote.
[9] Das, Bhagavan, *The Science of the Sacred Word*, Vol. I, p. 83.

active and dominant in man and in his corporeal existence, and little by little all parts of the etheric structure become vitally awake. Gradually the higher centres come into increased activity, and the emphasis of the force pouring through the body shifts to the centres above the diaphragm. The throat centre awakens and becomes the organ of creative work; the heart centre is vivified and the man becomes aware of his soul relationships, his group responsibilities and the inclusiveness of the life-soul. Finally the head centres awaken and another range of perceptions enters into his consciousness. He becomes aware of himself as a soul, integrated as a personality, and later still he becomes aware of the world of spirit, of divine life, of the unseen world of spirits, and of that "cloud of witnesses" who testify to the reality of the soul life.

One of the objectives of human evolution is to accomplish this. The centre at the base of the spine, the heart and head centres, must come into full functioning activity and thus, through a blending of the energy latent in matter itself and stored up in the centre at the base of the spine, of the energy of the soul, which has its seat in the heart, and of the energy of the spirit, centred in the head, bring the human being to the highest point of perfection. Through this fusion of energies he becomes an active expression of God,—spirit, soul, body, blended and united so that the body is indeed the vehicle for the soul, and that soul is indeed the expression of the will and purpose of the spirit.

What did Christ say when on earth? "He that hath seen me hath seen the Father." (John XIV:9). He said also, "He that believeth on Me, the works that I do shall he do also; and greater works than these shall he do; because I go unto My Father" (John XIV:12). He was the Soul incarnate in the body, revealing the Father, the Spirit, and through the mechanism of the body, demonstrating the powers of the soul, which, the Hindus claim, follow upon the awakening of the centres, and which they list as follows:

1. Anima ... the power to penetrate all bodies, and to bring the dead to life. Christ could pass unseen into rooms, and could raise the dead. (See Luke 24:36, Mark 16:14, John 20:19, John 11).

2. Mahima ... the power to include or make oneself large or to comprehend the universe. Christ knew all things. (Matt. 12:25, John 2:24, John 6:64.)

3. Laghima ... the power to make oneself light so that one could float in the air or walk on the water. Christ walked on the water (Matt. 14:25, 26, Mark 6:48).

4. Garima ... the power to make oneself heavy. There is no record in the Christian Scripture of Christ exercising this power.

5. Prapti ... the predicting of events (Christ foretold his crucifixion Matt. 26:2, Luke 24:7) and of the power to cure diseases (Christ healed hundreds, Matt. 12:15, 14:15), and of clairvoy-

ance and clairaudience. (Christ was both clairvoyant, John 1:48, and clairaudient, John 12:29.)

6. Prakamega . . . the power to preserve the body. Christ reappeared to His disciples after death with the same body, apparently, that they knew. (John 20:20-27).

7. Visitvan . . . the power of self control, the power to control animals, and people. All these Christ demonstrated, even to the control of the demon-possessed persons, and of the hogs who ran down a steep place into the sea (Matt. 8, Mark 5, Mark 9).

8. Ishatvan . . . the power of universal dominion. This is everywhere claimed for Christ, and is indicated by his being seated on the right hand of God.

And is the possession of these powers and the fulfilment of Christ's prophecy that we shall do these greater things, so contrary to what the West calls common sense? In the radio, we broadcast waves of sound and we time and amplify them, but after all we merely reenforce the sound waves which in their original subtle form, are pouring in upon us. What more natural than this, that man, who has constructed mechanical reenforcements, should himself become so sensitive as to pick up the sound waves unaided, and thus be termed clairaudient? And is not thought transference (which even the most skeptical must recognise) none other than a special kind of broadcasting? And so with other "miracles," is not the material world controlled by subtler forces and powers, and may not man learn in time to operate in the subtler field and thereby acquire dominance over the merely physical and material?

Such is the age-long belief of India—that through the development of the soul and spirit, through the awakening of all the centres, man comes to his maturity and his glory.

Chapter VII

CONCLUSION

In this book we have considered the two systems of psychology, the Eastern and the Western. Taken together we have a complete picture of man as a living soul, functioning through a certain mechanism. Part of this, the etheric body with its centres, is subtle, unseen and beyond the reach of our five senses, and another part is in the dense physical realm, namely the endocrine glands and the nervous system, which control the rest of the dense physical manifestation. These two parts, we believe, form one whole.

The soul is always the great reality, the expression of the one life, which is made up of the etheric and dense bodies. It is the soul force playing upon and functioning through the etheric body which evolves the specialised centres in that body, and which in turn acts upon the dense physical.

The question which appeals most strongly to the Western mind is how to achieve greater efficiency in operation. Man, the soul, is limited in his operating efficiency by the condition of his instrument. If the glands, nervous system and the etheric body with its centres are out of adjustment and not functioning properly, man, the soul, must repair or heal them. It is only because man is essen-

Conclusion

tially a living soul that we can even conceive of his glands as not functioning properly, much less proceed to study, correct and perfect them.

Work directly upon the glands and the nerve centres through the use of medicines and by other means is essentially repair work, and is limited to the highest state of those particular glands and nerve centres originally created by the particular man in question. The same is equally, and if anything, more emphatically true of the centres in the etheric body which can be affected by certain Oriental practices of breathing, mantras and posture. Such practices are most dangerous, often, indeed, leading to insanity. Eventually, it is to be hoped, we shall have sufficient knowledge and experience to work with intelligence directly upon the centres and thus be able to control more effectively the neuroses and glands of the physical body.

Three theories apparently emerge as the result of our investigation, and form a triple hypothesis to account for man as an organism, demonstrating life, self-consciousness and intelligent purpose.

The first is: *As a man's glands and nervous system, so is he.* His temperament, natural qualities and intelligent handling of his life experiences and of his environment are determined by his endocrine system. So says the West.

The second is: *As a man's centres, so is he.* The quiescence or the activity of certain focal points of energy in the human, etheric body, determine his character, his method of expression, his type and also the tenure of his body. His activities on the physical plane are entirely dependent upon the qualities of force flowing through his centres. So says the East.

The third is: *The glands and neuroses as well as the centres are conditioned by the control or lack of control exerted by the soul.*

It might be argued that we have only succeeded in pushing the whole matter back into the realms of the unseen and the unprovable. But is this really so? Have not many factors now accepted as realities emerged from the speculations and vague hypotheses of the past ages? Has not what was regarded as unprovable in the past been proved and demonstrated in the present age? Might it not be possible to apply a technique and employ a method which may in time suffice, through the mass of direct available evidence, to give us a clearer perception of the factors which are at present so obscure to us?

The West comes forward as we have seen with its facts concerning the structure. Man's mechanism is determined by his endocrine system plus the nervous system, the response apparatus. Can we approach the subject from this standpoint and by a treatment of the human glands produce perfection of the human body and thus eventually lead man out into the full light of the soul? Can divinity be unfolded through physical means? Or, accepting the Eastern position that the centres are the mediums of expression for the soul, and responsible for the building and control of the body, through the nervous system and the glands, can we investigate and apply a recognisably dangerous method and work directly on or through the centres?

Is there a third way by means of which we can avoid the purely physical approach and also the danger of awakening the centres prematurely? May it not be possible to arrive at a solution and a method which will give the soul the full use of its instrument, and produce that perfect interplay between soul and body which a right activity of the centres is claimed to bring about?

There is a way whereby man can ascertain that he is really a soul, and therefore is able to control his instrument of expression, the threefold lower nature, the sum-total of psychical and mental states. Through this method it is possible to bring about a union of the wisdom of the East and the knowledge of the West, so that the best aspects of each system can be available to mankind as a whole.

In considering the possibility of man discovering his soul, there must be, to start with, a willingness to accept an hypothesis, for hypotheses have always been the starting point for knowledge. We assume then, as a working hypothesis that man is a soul and possesses a body, and that there is a unifying medium linking these two in the form of an energy body.

Those who have sought to ascertain the fact of the existence of the soul and of its vitalising apparatus hitherto can be divided into two groups. There are the mystics who have employed aspiration and emotion, plus physical means, and there are those who are more purely mental in caliber, and who have utilised the intellect and the mind, in order to arrive at spiritual knowledge. This long line of knowers of God have used different terminologies, but it is immaterial for our purpose whether they call the soul the self, the Beloved, the One, or God, or Christ. The mystic flagellated and misused his body through fasting and over-discipline. He thus reduced the claims of the fleshly appetites. To this he added an intense devotion for the Beloved and a longing for the Vision. At the close of years of strenuous exercise he found that which he sought, and was united with that Beloved.

The second group employed the reason and practiced mind control, plus stern emotional and physical control. Through the one-pointedness of their search they, too, found reality and came into a wide consciousness of the eternal plan, arriving at union with the Universal Soul.

Both groups bear testimony to the truth of the existence of the Soul, but, limited by their peculiar bent and method, their testimony is one-sided. One is too visionary, mystical and emotional; the other too academic, intellectual and form-building. Now, through the wide dissemination of human knowledge and the close intercourse existing between minds through the medium of literature, the spoken word and travel, the time has come when a fusion is, for the first time, generally possible, and, from the past conclusions of the philosophers and saints of both hemispheres, we should be able to work out a system and a method which will be for our day and generation the mode of spiritual achievement.

It becomes therefore practical for certain initial steps to be taken and these might be summarised as follows:

(a) A sane treatment of the physical body, utilising the knowledge of the West, particularly with reference to preventive medicine and the general health of the endocrine system.

(b) An intellectual understanding and application of the basic facts of modern psychology and a sane psycho-analysis, thus arriving at a knowledge of the mechanism, mental, emotional and physical, through which the soul seeks expression.

(c) A recognition of the fact that, as the physical body is an automaton, responsive to and controlled by the desires and the emotional nature, so these emotional states of consciousness (extending all the way from love of food to love of God) may be controlled by the reasoning mind.

(d) Growing out of all this will come a study of the laws of mind, and thus the relationship between the mind and the brain may be understood and utilised.

When these four points are grasped and their effect is felt in man's personality, we shall have the integrated and coordinated organism; the structure can then be regarded as ready for direction by the soul. The above stages must be understood, not as proceeding sequentially, but as going forward simultaneously. It is also apparent that perfect intellectual knowledge of the soul and of the world which that soul reveals is only possible to the man who has this outlined equipment. A sense of God, an appreciation of the true and beautiful, and a contact with the mystical vision is at all times possible to those whose heart centre is awake and functioning. Such Lovers of God have existed through the ages; they feel, sense, love and adore, but the link between soul, mind and brain is lacking. When to this mystical equipment there is added the intellectual, then the head centre is awakened, the pineal gland is no longer in an atrophied condition, but is known to be the seat of the soul and of the directing spiritual will. When both these centres are awakened we have the great outstanding spiritual personalities who work with consecrated heart and brain and set their seal on world thought. Hitherto the way of the mystic has been the way of the majority, and the way of the intellect has been for the few. But the race is now at the stage where, basing its hypothesis upon the mystical experiences of the many, it can go forward from feeling and adoration to knowledge, and from love of God into knowledge of God.

Conclusion

This will be the case when the wisdom of the East is added to the knowledge of the West and the technique of the science of the soul is imposed upon our Western intellectual types. It is impossible to enlarge at length upon this technique. It might, however, be briefly described as being divided into eight stages which can be listed as follows:

1. Control of our relations to others, summed up under the word *harmlessness* which is defined in the East by the Five Commandments. These are: Harmlessness, truth to all beings, abstention from theft, from incontinence and from avarice.[1]

2. Purity of life as outlined in the Five Rules: Internal and external purification, contentment, fiery aspiration, spiritual reading and devotion to Ishvara (the divine Self).[2]

3. Poise.

4. Right control of the life force and hence direct action by the soul upon the etheric body. This control of energy and therefore of the centres and of the physical body is only possible after a man has achieved purity and poise. He is not permitted knowledge of the laws governing energy until such time as he has learned, through discipline, the control of the animal nature, and has reached a point where he is no longer swayed by moods and selfishness.

5. Abstraction. A term which covers the power to centre one's consciousness in the head and there

---
[1] Bailey, Alice A., *The Light of the Soul*, p. 184.
[2] Ibid., p. 187.

to function as a soul, or to withdraw the outgoing consciousness from things objective and tangible, and so turn it within.

6. Attention or concentration. This is one-pointed living, and involves also the bringing the mind into activity in the place of the emotions. Thus the emotional and physical man are controlled by the focussed mind.

7. Meditation is prolonged attention or concentration and gives the power to focus the mind upon the soul and its concerns. This produces radical changes in the organism and substantiates the truth of the statement that, "as a man thinketh, so is he."

8. Contemplation is the act of the soul in its own realm as it looks out over the forms and contacts the energies found in the fifth or spiritual kingdom in nature. This act is followed by the pouring down into the brain (by way of the controlled mind) of soul knowledge and energy. This activity of the soul produces what has been called illumination: it brings about the energising of the entire man and awakens the centres in proper rhythm and progression.

This consciously directed spiritual energy playing through the vital body and the centres should, it is claimed, bring physical man and the endocrine system eventually into such a condition that we should have perfect health and therefore a perfect apparatus for soul expression. In this way we are taught that man can arrive at a definite knowledge of the soul, and can know himself to be "the deeper

Being," able to use his mechanism with definite purpose, and thus function as a soul.

A study of the lives of the great mystics, saints and adepts of both hemispheres will give much information about the phenomenal effects resulting from following the above method, even after we have eliminated much that savours of hallucination and psychopathic conditions. Forms of clairvoyance, of prevision and of telepathic communication, clairaudient faculties and the peculiar power to psychometrise are frequently seen. It should be remembered, however, that all these powers have their spiritual manifestations and also their lower. A. E. Powell says:

"There are, roughly, two main kinds of clairvoyance, the lower and the higher. The lower variety appears sporadically in undeveloped people, such as the savages of Central Africa, and is a sort of massive sensation vaguely belonging to the whole etheric body, rather than an exact and definite sense-perception communicated through a specialized organ. It is practically beyond man's control. The Etheric Double being in exceedingly close relationship with the nervous system, any action on one of them reacts speedily on the other. In the lower clairvoyance the corresponding nervous disturbance is almost entirely in the sympathetic system.

In more developed races the vague sensitiveness usually disappears as the mental faculties are developed. Later on, when the spiritual man begins to unfold, he regains clairvoyant power. This time, however, the faculty is precise and exact, under the control of the will, and exercised through a sense-organ. Any nervous action set up is almost exclusively in the cerebro-spinal system.

The lower forms of psychism are most frequent in animals and very unintelligent human beings. Hysterical and ill-regulated psychism is due to the small development of the brain and the dominance of the sympathetic system, the large nucleated ganglionic cells in this system containing a very large proportion of etheric matter, and thus being easily affected by the coarser astral vibrations." [3]

It has been frequently noticed that cats and dogs and low-grade human beings can frequently see and hear that which the normal and more intelligent person fails to register. This faculty is, however, unconscious, and the man is frequently an hallucinated victim. The saint and seer likewise see and hear, but their powers are utilised at will and are entirely under their control. A large field for investigation in these matters lies open to all psychical investigators, and when the hypothesis of the vital body and the centres is admitted, much real knowledge may come.

It is claimed by the teachers of the Eastern science of the soul that the awakening of the various centres reveals states of subtler matter than the physical. It is mainly, however, with the centres above the diaphragm that the spiritual man concerns himself, conferring, as they do, such powers as spiritual perception, correct understanding and interpretation of one's fellow-men, so that, like Christ, we know what is in man, and can grasp why

---
[3] Powell, A. E., *The Etheric Double*, pp. 102, 103.

a man is what he is, and acts as he does. The force of inspiration, the highest power of them all, works out as the inspiring of creative work through the medium of the throat centre, and of humanitarian enterprises through the medium of the heart centre.

The second effect claimed by this group is the transference of the force below the diaphragm to the centres above. Through evolution and the effect of meditation work a man is able to function consciously through his three major centres, (head heart and throat) leaving the three lower centres, (the base of the spine, sacral centre and solar plexus) to carry on their normal function of energising the body automatically, so that the digestive apparatus and the reproductive system and certain aspects of the nervous mechanism can carry forward their work. According to this theory, the majority of people live "below the diaphragm" and the life force is centred in the purely animal and sensory life; the sex life and the emotional life are dominant, and all the force flowing into and through the sacral centre and the solar plexus go to the stimulation of certain physiological and lower psychical processes. As man evolves, however, the direction of the force changes. We have seen that the force is dual, being partially life force and partially soul force, one expressing itself through the blood and the other through the nervous system. The life force aspect continues to carry forward its function of vitalising and empowering all the organs and structures of the body, but the soul force, hitherto relatively quiescent, begins to turn upwards. The soul force in the centre at the base of the spine is carried to the head via the spinal canal, passing through each centre in turn, gathering increasing soul energy at each point.

The psychological effects of this transfer of consciousness are interesting. When the soul is "enthroned" (as the scientific Oriental books put it) in the head, it attracts upward to itself, through the power of its magnetism, the force latent at the base of the spine. Thus is produced the complete blending of spiritual energy and the force in matter itself through the attractive energy of the soul. This is what is meant by the arousing of the Kundalini power and it should be done by the magnetism of the dominant soul, and not by meditation on any specific centre or by conscious action on the force of matter.

The soul energy of the sacral centre must be carried to the highest creative centre, the throat. The emphasis will then be laid on creative work carried forward for the sake of the group and not on the active sex life of the man concerned.

The energy of the solar plexus centre has, equally, to be transferred and carried to the heart, and the consciousness then is no longer self-centred and purely selfish, but the man becomes group-conscious and inclusive in his attitude to people and to life. He is no longer antagonistic and exclusive. He knows and understands. He pities, loves and serves. There is a wide field for research once this relationship between centre and centre, and between centre and glands, is grasped; the effects, physiological as well as psychical, will warrant close study.

It is interesting also to note another claim made by students of the Ageless Wisdom. When man has reached a fairly high state of evolution the throat centre is functioning and he is beginning to take his place in the work of the world; he has a definite output in some field of world activity. His personality then may be regarded as organised, and he can be deemed to have reached his maturity. The psychologists tell us that the pituitary body is the seat of the emotional and mental characteristics. In one lobe the reasoning mind has its seat, whilst the other is responsible for the imaginative emotional faculties, and the power to visualise. In man, with creative power, and, therefore, with a developed personality, the two lobes of the pituitary body are equal to the demand, and from them can be deduced the status of the material aspect, the mechanism through which the soul moves and expresses itself. This gland is concerned with the centre between the eyebrows. This centre is negative to the centre in the head which is responsive to the energy of the Soul. When through conformity to the outlined technique, the soul assumes control, energises the head centre and brings the pineal gland from an atrophied to a functioning condition as in the days of childhood, the positive aspect begins to play its part. A relationship is set up between the negative centre and its counterpart, the pituitary body, and the positive centre and its counterpart, the pineal gland. As time proceeds, it is claimed, a magnetic field is set up, soul and body meet, the father and mother come into relationship and the soul is brought to the birth in the consciousness of man. This is the birth of the Christ in the House of God, and the coming into being of the true man; of this the sex organs and their reproductive activities on the physical plane are the outer concretised symbol. The perversions of sex magic so widely prevalent are a distortion of this true spiritual union or fusion between the two centres of energy in the head, which are, in their turn, figurative of the relation between soul and body. Sex magic relegates the process to the centre below the diaphragm and to a relation between two persons on the physical plane. The true process is carried forward within a man's own nature, centred in the head and the relation is between the soul and the body, instead of between man and woman.

Another effect claimed for this relationship between the two head centres and their corresponding glands is that the interplay between the two produces the shining forth of a light. There is much corroborative evidence in this connection in the Scriptures of the world, including Christ's injunction to His followers to "let their light shine." There is cumulative evidence also in the lives of

Conclusion

the mystics, who again and again in their writings bear testimony to a light that has been seen. I sent out a letter to a group of students (who have been studying meditation for several years) asking if they were aware of any phenomena of interest as the result of their work. The letter was not sent to neurotics and visionary types, but to men and women of good standing in the business, artistic and literary fields, and with accomplishment to their credit. Seventy-five per cent testified to seeing a light in the head. Were they hallucinated? Were they the victims of their imaginations? What was it they saw? and constantly see?

An interesting field for investigation lies here also, and the results may have a basis in the fact, now recognised by science, that light is matter, and matter is light. When the soul is functioning and the man has achieved conscious union with that soul, he may then, through the extra stimulation involved, become aware of the light of the etheric body at its main point of junction with the physical body at the most important centre in the body, the head centre. Professor Bazzoni says:

"We have seen that all forms of matter on the earth are made up of 92 different kinds of atoms grouped into molecules which, taken together in countless millions, form all of the bodies which we see about us and indeed for that matter, our own bodies. Now, any one of these 92 kinds of atoms when stimulated in certain ways well known to science can be made to give off light—generally colored light—and the nature of this light is peculiar and characteristic for each of the 92 atoms." [4]

Does this throw any light on our problem, provided the hypothesis of an etheric body is admitted? Is the halo around the heads of saints and of deity in all the ancient pictures of both hemispheres an indication that the artists knew they were painting illuminated men in the physical as well as in the spiritual sense? These things should be investigated, and either proved or disproved.

The possibility of unifying the two great schools of thought which seek to account for the unit man in terms of Western achievement and of Eastern philosophy based on a technique of soul control is therefore in the nature of an experiment. Given the willingness to accept what the Western student regards as hypothetical and given an open mind, what can be done of specific and practical import to demonstrate as truth or to reject as false the arguments put forward in this book?

Maeterlinck quotes Herbert Spencer to the effect that:

"Perpetually to construct ideas requiring the utmost stretch of our faculties and perpetually to find that such ideas must be abandoned as futile imaginations, may realize to us more fully than any other course the greatness of that which we vainly strive to grasp. . . . By continually seeking to know and being continually thrown back with a deepened conviction of the impossibility of knowing, we may keep alive the conscious-

---
[4] Bazzoni, C. B., *Kernels of the Universe*, p. 31.

ness that it is alike our highest wisdom and our highest duty to regard that through which all things exist as the Unknowable." [5]

But may it not be possible, however, to clear our vision somewhat and "deepening our conviction," arrive at a better understanding of the forms and aspects which veil that unknowable Essential Reality in whose Body we "live and move and have our being?"

Granted that it is the phenomenal world, whether it is the human family we are considering, or the forms visioned and contacted in the Kingdom of the Soul, it may be eventually proved true that, progressively, the forms (as they mount in the scale of being) may reveal to us expanding truths about that Essential Life. As the mechanism develops and improves so may our concepts of Divinity. Edward Carpenter expresses this idea in the following words:

"Dr. Frazer, in the conclusion of his great work, *The Golden Bough*, bids farewell to his readers with the following words: 'The laws of Nature are merely hypotheses devised to explain that ever-shifting phantasmagoria of thought which we dignify with the high-sounding names of the World and the Universe. In the last analysis magic, religion and science are nothing but theories (of thought); and as science has supplanted its predecessors, so it may hereafter itself be superseded by some more perfect hypothesis, perhaps by some perfectly different way of looking at phenomena, of registering the shadows on the screen—of

---

[5] Maeterlinck, Maurice, *The Light Beyond*, p. 95.

which we in this generation can form no idea.' I imagine Dr. Frazer is right in thinking that 'a way of looking at phenomena' different from the way of science, may some day prevail. But I think this change will come, not so much by the growth of Science itself or the extension of its 'hypotheses,' as by a growth and expansion of the human *heart* and a change in its psychology and powers of perception." [6]

Maeterlinck sums this up very succinctly when he says: "It behooves us therefore to clear away conceptions that emanate only from our body, even as the mists that veil the daylight from our sight emanate only from the lowlands. Pascal has said, once and for all: 'The narrow limits of our being conceal infinity from our view.'" [7]

Practical suggestions must be made in the attempt to disprove the supernatural (if it might be so expressed) and prove that the subjective states to which the mystic and seer testify are simply demonstrations of natural forces and powers. These powers man has failed as yet to recognise and control, just as he failed centuries ago to cognise those forces which he is now able, to some extent at least, to understand and use, and which are the glory of our present civilisation. Let us prove one of these soul powers to be a fact in nature and the portals of a new world will open before humanity. Dr. Leary appreciates this when he says:

---

[6] Carpenter, Edward, *Pagan and Christian Creeds; Their Origin and Meaning*, p. 278.
[7] Maeterlinck, Maurice, *The Light Beyond*, p. 73.

Conclusion 147

"It is somehow felt that there are some qualities, some traits at least of some personalities, which cannot be accounted for in terms of the activity of any physical structure. Nor is this an unimportant point which can be summarily dismissed as mere superstition; it is too widespread, too highly charged with emotion, too much shared in even by some psychologists to be ignored. And it is worth while once more mentioning, if there be any such traits, spiritual or what not, which by definition or assumption are not based on structure, the admission of even the smallest and seemingly most unimportant of these will inevitably and completely negative the whole field of science, for determinism to be true determinism must be completely so." [8]

First it should be possible to found a laboratory where the claims of the student of the Oriental philosophy in connection with the vitalising soul can be substantiated or proved false. The phenomena of death can be studied from the angle of the withdrawal of the soul. The radiations from the human body have, of course, received attention, but specific investigation of the spine and its relation to the centres is as yet a new field of study, though Dr. Baraduc of the Sorbonne, Paris, did some interesting work in this connection forty-five years ago. His book, *L'Ame Vitale,* is suggestive, though conjectural, and his contentions need substantiating.

The whole subject of the vital body and its effects on the nervous system and the glands open up an immense field for study; whilst the relation-

---

[8] Leary, Daniel H., Ph.D., *Modern Psychology: Normal and Abnormal,* pp. 191, 192.

ship of the ether-body of man not only to his nerve apparatus but to the planetary etheric body or the ether in which he, as an organism, has his place, is yet an untouched field.

Secondly it should be possible to gather testimony as to the fact and nature of the light in the head to which so many testify.

The recent spectacular experiments into the nature of telepathy are tending in the right direction, but this technique of telepathy is as yet in its infancy; much will be revealed when a distinction is made between communication from mind to mind, which is mental telepathy, and that much rarer form of communication between soul and soul and between soul and brain. This latter form has been called inspiration and has brought into being the Scriptures and the so-called "inspired" writings of the world, and has guided the mental processes of the great inventors and scientists, poets and artists.

Telepathy and inspiration are as dependent upon the individual human etheric body and its relation to the universal ether as is light itself or the radio. They bear witness to this subtler world of spirit and of soul.

Pupin in the epilogue to *The New Reformation* says:

"The creative power of the soul is the only guide in our attempts to decipher the meaning of this ultra-material substance. It furnishes the most reliable standard of comparing the soul of one man with the soul of another man and with that of lower animals.

This comparison, resembling, to some extent, the scientific methods of quantitative measurement, has been going on ever since civilization began. The procedure of this inquiry is in many ways equivalent to the scientific method of inquiry by observation, experiment and calculation; what it lacks in precision it makes up by its vast number of trials and errors extending over many centuries of qualitative measurements by careful comparison. It resulted in the universal verdict, that not only is the soul of man far superior to the animal soul, but that this difference is immeasurably greater than the difference in their bodily structures. The comparison revealed also an element in this difference which towers high above all the other differentiating elements; it is the *spiritual* element. The creative power of the human soul has created a new world in human consciousness; it is the spiritual world." [9]

Among other possible avenues of research is the carrying forward of the work of Dr. Kilner with the human aura, which he has embodied in his book, *The Human Atmosphere.* Still further lines of investigation into the supernormal powers have been well summed up for us in a recent statement from an Australian periodical called *The Federal Independent,* and from which two paragraphs are here quoted:

"New light on Christ's walking on the waters was thrown recently by a scientist who has been making a special study of Einstein's newest theory of relativity. As a result of his investigations Professor H. H. Sheldon says that he may find it possible to assert that the Biblical narrative at which the sceptics have so long

---
[9] Pupin, Michael, *The New Reformation,* pp. 264, 265.

mocked is a fact explicable by scientific laws. 'The miracle can be accepted by the most sceptical minds as soon as they recognize the fact that the basic laws of relativistic mechanics and of electricity can be reduced to one formula, and that the power of electromagnetism can influence and completely control gravitation,' said Professor Sheldon. According to Einstein's latest mathematical theory there is only one substance and one universal law containing electric and gravitational components, both of which are united into a single formula, and each of which influences the other. Dr. Sheldon now believes that as a result of this discovery such things as keeping aeroplanes aloft without engines or material support, and stepping out of a window into the air without fear of falling, are avenues of investigation easily suggested. 'If this theory stands up as a proof that electricity and gravitation are virtually the same, we can actually isolate ourselves from the force of gravitation,' he declared. In actual proof of these seemingly incredible possibilities, Dr. Sheldon showed how a bar of permalloy, which is usually sensitive to magnetism, will remain suspended seemingly by air alone, if a magnet is placed underneath it.

In the light of Einstein's new theory, therefore, it may be that Christ's freedom from the accepted laws of gravitation, which would have forced Him to sink as soon as His feet touched the surface of the sea, was due to a prodigious amount of electro-magnetism in His own body, and from a force springing from the strength of His personality and vitality. In all the paintings of Christ He is shown with a halo about His head. Once this halo was regarded as the product of His disciples' overwrought imaginations. But during the last few years science, along with many students of psychic phenomena, has shown by means of actual experiments that every human being has an aura which

Conclusion 151

strongly resembles that refulgence emanating from any powerful electric machine.

Such a statement is a further proof that science is rapidly crossing the border-line separating things material from things spiritual. Once we realize that the knowledge of higher laws can overcome the resistance of lower laws, then we shall enter our true spiritual heritage."

We stand expectantly awaiting the dawn of that day when religion will stand upon a scientific basis and the truths to which the ages bear witness will be substantiated and proven, for, as Dr. Pupin further tells us:

"Yes, God's spiritual realities are invisible, but they are illustrated and made intelligible by the physical realities revealed in the physical things which are made. According to this interpretation of the Apostle's words the physical and the spiritual realities supplement each other. They are the two terminals of the same realities, one terminal residing in the human soul, and the other in the things of the external world. Here is one of the fundamental reasons why Science and Religion supplement each other. They are the two pillars of the portal through which the human soul enters the world where the divinity resides." [10]

Then there will emerge a new race, with new capacities, new ideals, new concepts about God and matter, about life and spirit. Through that race and through the humanity of the future there will be seen not only a mechanism and a structure, but a soul, an entity, who, using the mechanism, will

---
[10] Pupin, Michael, *The New Reformation*, p. 272.

manifest its own nature, which is love, wisdom and intelligence.

Science has even recognised this ultimate possibility and noted that the trend of the evolutionary process is towards a more perfect adaptation between the form and the life. Everywhere throughout creation a purpose is working out, a will towards perfection is manifesting. That purpose and that will are controlled by love and wisdom and those two types of energy—the purpose of spirit and the attractive force of the soul—are intelligently applied to the perfecting of the matter aspect. Spirit, soul and body—a divine triplicity—manifest in the world and will carry all forward towards a consummation that is pictured for us in the Scriptures of the world in a wealth of imagery, of color and of form. Browning's vision of this truth and his expression of it will sum up for us the results of our study and will be a fitting close for this essay:

> "—and God renews
> His ancient rapture. Thus He dwells in all,
> From life's minute beginnings, up at last
> To man—the consummation of this scheme
> Of being, the completion of this sphere
> Of life; whose attributes had here and there
> Been scattered o'er the visible world before,
> Asking to be combined, dim fragments meant
> To be united in some wondrous whole,
> Imperfect qualities throughout creation,
> Suggesting some one creature yet to make,
> Some point where all these scattered rays should meet

Conclusion

Convergent in the faculties of man. . . .
When all the race is perfected alike
As man, that is; all tended to mankind,
And, man produced, all has its end thus far;
But in completed man begins anew
A tendency to God. Prognostics told
Man's near approach; so in man's self arise
August anticipations, symbols, types
Of a dim splendor ever on before
In that eternal circle life pursues.
For men begin to pass their nature's bound,
And find new hopes and cares which fast supplant
Their proper joys and griefs; they grow too great
For narrow creeds of right and wrong, which fade
Before the unmeasured thirst for good; while peace
Rises within them ever more and more.
Such men are even now upon the earth,
Serene amid the half-formed creatures round." [11]

---
[11] Browning, Robert, *Paracelsus*.

APPENDIX

Note I

(On Chapter IV)

The following extract from a recent publication puts the question of the soul in another way, and perhaps, will give us some idea of the trend of modern Western thought regarding it.

The phrase religious insight is in itself vague. Is it not possible to give the phrase a definite content without departing from the critical attitude? One may be helped to such a definition by asking oneself what element has tended to fall out of the life of the modern man with the decline of the traditional disciplines. According to Mr. Walter Lippmann, the conviction the modern man has lost is that "there is an immortal essence presiding like a king over his appetites." But why abandon the affirmation of such an "essence" or higher will, to the mere traditionalist? Why not affirm it first of all as a psychological fact, one of the immediate data of consciousness, a perception so primordial that, compared with it, the deterministic denials of man's moral freedom are only a metaphysical dream? One would thus be in a position to perform a swift flanking movement on the behaviourists and other naturalistic psychologists who are to be regarded at present as among the chief enemies of human nature. One might at the same time be in a fair way to escape from the modernist dilemma and become a thoroughgoing and complete modern.

The philosophers have often debated the question of the priority of will or intellect in man. The quality of will that I am discussing and that rightly deserves to be accounted superrational, has, however, been associated in traditional Christianity not primarily with man's will, but with God's will in the form of grace. The theologians have indulged in many unprofitable subtleties apropos of grace. One cannot afford, however, as has been the modern tendency, to discard the psychological truth of the doctrine along with these subtleties. The higher will must simply be accepted as a mystery that may be studied in its practical effects, but that, in its ultimate nature, is incapable of formulation. Herein the higher will is not peculiar. "All things," according to the scholastic maxim, "end in a mystery." The man of science is increasingly willing to grant that the reality behind the phenomena he is studying not only eludes him, but must in the nature of the case ever elude him. He no longer holds, for example, as his more dogmatic forbears of the nineteenth century incline to do, that the mechanistic hypothesis, valuable as it has proved itself to be as a laboratory technique, is absolutely true; its truth is, he admits, relative and provisional.

The person who declines to turn the higher will to account until he is sure he has grasped its ultimate nature is very much on a level with the man who should refuse to make practical use of electrical energy until he is certain he has an impeccable theory of electricity. Negatively one may say of the higher will, without overstepping the critical attitude, that it is not the absolute, nor again the categorical imperative; not the organic and still less the mechanical; finally, not the "ideal" in the current sense of that term. Positively one may define it as the higher immediacy that is known in its relation to the lower immediacy—the merely temperamental man with his impressions and emotions and expansive desires—as a power of vital control. Failure to exercise this control is the spiritual indolence that is for both Christian and Buddhist a chief source, if not the chief source, of evil. Though Aristotle, after the Greek fashion, gives the primacy not to will but to mind, the power of which I have been speaking is surely related to his "energy of soul," the form of activity distinct from a mere outer working, deemed by him appropriate for the life of leisure that he proposes as the goal of a liberal education. . . . The energy of soul that has served on the humanistic level for mediation appears on the religious level in the form of meditation. Religion may of course mean a great deal more than meditation. At the same time humanistic mediation that has the support of meditation may correctly be said to have a religious background. Mediation and meditation are after all only different stages in the same ascending "path" and should not be arbitrarily separated.

> Article: Humanism: An Essay on Definition by Irving Babbitt, pp. 39-41. From Humanism and America: Essays on the Outlook of Modern Civilization, edited by Norman Foerster.

Note II
(On Chapter VII)

It has been interesting to note the spread of hyperthyroidism at this time, and various troubles connected with the thyroid gland. May not these conditions be a substantiation of the Oriental theory? Many people from force of circumstances and strained economic conditions are leading an abnormal sex life, and are celibate. Others, from what may be a mistaken idea of spiritual demands, reject the normal marriage state, and pledge themselves to a life of celibacy. Owing to these conditions the force is raised to the center which is its goal, and reaches the throat. The whole condition being abnormal and the man or woman being as yet emotionally centered, and the mental equipment (so necessary in true creative work) being relatively mediocre, there is no ability to use this creative power, and there ensues an over-stimulation of the thyroid gland. Several such cases have been noted by us and seem to substantiate this position. This is one direction in which investigation and use of the scientific method of massing evidence to prove or disprove an hypothesis would appear to be capable of application. In the aggregate of cases and of testimony, light on this matter may appear. When the transfer is normal and not premature the outcome is along the line of recognised creative work, literature, the drama, music and the arts in general.

BIBLIOGRAPHY

THE GLANDS—

The Glands of Destiny, Ivo G. Cobb, M.D.
The Glands Regulating Personality, Louis Berman, M.D.
Our Glands and Our Evolvement, M. W. Kapp, M.D.
The Pineal Gland, Frederick Tilney, M.D.
The Third Eye. (Pineal and Pituitary Bodies.) T. P. C. Barnard, M.D.
Your Mysterious Glands, H. H. Rubin, M.D.

PSYCHOLOGY:—

About Ourselves, H. A. Overstreet
Behaviorism, John B. Watson
History of Psychology, W. B. Pillsbury, Ph.D.
Mind and Matter, C. E. M. Joad, B.A.
Modern Psychology, Normal and Abnormal, Daniel Bell Leary, Ph.D.
Psychologies of 1925, Carl Murchison, Ed.
Why We Behave Like Human Beings, George A. Dorsey, Ph.D., LL.D.

THE CENTRES:—

The Bhagavad-Gita
The Chakras, C. W. Leadbeater
The Etheric Double, Maj. Arthur E. Powell
Hatha Yoga
Hatha Yoga Pradipika
Indian Philosophy. (2 Vols.), S. Radhakrishnan
The Kathnopanishad
The Kenopanishad
The Light of the Soul, Alice A. Bailey

The Mysterious Kundalini, Vesant G. Rele
Nature's Finer Forces, Rama Prasad
Outlines of Indian Philosophy, P. T. Srinivasa Iyengar
The Philosophy of the Upanishads, Paul Deussen
The Prashnopanishad
Principles of Tantra (2 Vols.), Arthur Avalon (Sir John Woodroffe)
Raja Yoga, Swami Vivekananda
The Serpent Power, Arthur Avalon (Sir John Woodroffe)
Shakti and Shakta, Sir John Woodroffe (Arthur Avalon)
Shatchakra Nirupanamm
Shiv-Samhita
Yoga Sutras of Patanjali
Yoga Vasitha

GENERAL:—

Creative Understanding, Count Hermann Keyserling
Encyclopedia Britannica (13th Edition)
Ether and Reality, Sir Oliver Lodge
The Garland of Letters, Sir John Woodroffe (Arthur Avalon)
The Human Atmosphere, Walter J. Kilner, B.A., M.B.
In Search of the Soul (2 Vols.), Bernard Hollander, M.D.
Kernels of the Universe, C. B. Bazzoni
The Light Beyond, Maurice Maeterlinck
Man and His Becoming, René Guénon
The Mansions of Philosophy, Will Durant
Metaphysical Foundations of Modern Physical Science, Edwin Arthur Burtt, Ph.D.
Mysteries of the Soul, Richard Muller-Freienfels

The New Reformation, Michael Pupin
On the Threshold of the Unseen, Sir William Barrett
Pagan and Christian Creeds, Edward Carpenter
Religion, Edward Scribner Ames
The Science of Peace, Bhagavan Das
The Science of the Sacred Word, Bhagavan Das
Self, Its Body and Freedom, William E. Hocking
The Strength of Religion as Shown by Science, E. de M. Sajous
Studies in the Bhagavad-Gita, The Dreamer

THE GREAT INVOCATION

From the point of Light within the Mind of God
   Let light stream forth into the minds of men.
   Let Light descend on Earth.

From the point of Love within the Heart of God
   Let love stream forth into the hearts of men.
   May Christ return to Earth.

From the centre where the Will of God is known
   Let purpose guide the little wills of men —
   The purpose which the Masters know and serve.

From the centre which we call the race of men
   Let the Plan of Love and Light work out
   And may it seal the door where evil dwells.

Let Light and Love and Power restore the Plan on Earth.

"The above Invocation or Prayer does not belong to any person or group but to all Humanity. The beauty and the strength of this Invocation lies in its simplicity, and in its expression of certain central truths which all men, innately and normally, accept — the truth of the existence of a basic intelligence to Whom we vaguely give the name of God; the truth that behind all outer seeming, the motivating power of the universe is Love; the truth that a great Individuality came to earth, called by Christians, the Christ, and embodied that love so that we could understand; the truth that both love and intelligence are effects of what is called the will of God; and finally the self-evident truth that only through *humanity* itself can the Divine Plan work out."

ALICE A. BAILEY

Training for new age discipleship is provided by the *Arcane School*. The principles of the Ageless Wisdom are presented through esoteric meditation, study and service as a *way of life*.

Write to the publishers for information.

INDEX

)straction, definition and need for, 135–136

{renals, functions, 48–50

:asha, oriental teaching, 93, 94, 96–97

ma, consciousness, 116

man, concepts, 82–83, 102–103, 104

tention in science of soul, 136

ra, human, 149, 150–151

naviour, field, factors three, 33–34

agavad Gita—
)sychology of life and energy, 27
reatise on soul, 82

od—
nedium of expression, 103
elation to activity of glands, 39

lily existence, maintenance equipment, 110

ly, dense, activity production, means, 110–111

in—
onstitution, 117
ortex, 103
1pouring of soul knowledge and energy, 136

wning, Robert, on man, 91, 152–153

tres of force. *See* Force centres.

kras. *See* Force centres.

ist—
rth in head, 142
)wers, 125–126
alking on water, discussion, 149–150

rvoyance, types, 137–138

:entration in science of soul, 136

sciousness—
aracterising nervous system, 26
pression, 117
entical with Atma, 116
anifested world from, 57
organ of, 116
hicle of soul, 109, 122

Contemplation of soul, definition, 136

Courage mechanism, 49–50

Danger of awakening centres prematurely, avoidance, 131

Determinism active, of western psychology, 20–22

Einstein theory, application, 149–150

Electricity, identical with gravitation, 150

Electromagnetism, control of gravitation, 150

Endocrine glands. *See* Glands.

Energy—
nuclei, seven, 55
of Self, adaptation to structure used, possibility, 28–29
Oriental views, 54–59
pranic, conveyance, means, 110–111

Equipment, structure and motivating energy mutually interdependent, 18

Ether, universal medium, 59–67

Etheric body—
direct action of soul on, 135
existence, fact, establishment, necessity, 55
light in head, 143–144
theory, 54, 71

Evolution, effects, 123–127, 139–140

Evolutionary—
process, trend, 152
status of individual, effects, 119–120, 139–142

Force—
centres, seven, 108–127
transference from below diaphragm, 139–141

Form—
etheric body, 54
production, 109

163

INDEX

Glands—
   activity, due to centres, 121, 122
   description, 38–39
   functions, 39, 40–41
   location, relation to location of centres, 120
   names, location, and secretion, 40
   relation to personality, 51–52
   system importance, 19–20, 34–38
   See also names of specific glands.
Gonads, functions, 50
Gravitation control, 150

Harmlessness, five commandments, 135
Head centres, two, interplay, 142–143
Health, perfect, production, 136
Human behaviour and personality, factors, 33–40

Ida and Pingala, 117
Illumination, production and results, 136
Inspiration, dependence on etheric body, 148
Introspectionists and mentalists, 23–24

Kundalini, teaching regarding, 99, 100, 106

Life—
   force—
      contact with physical body, seven points, 110–111
      right control, 135
      transmission to physical body, 110–111
   relation to substance, Oriental view, 57
Light—
   in head, 142, 143, 148, 150–151
   nature of, 143

Man—
   a living soul, 128–129
   as organism, triple hypothesis accounting for, 129–130

Matter—
   energising, means, 108
   light, 143
   relation to spirit, Oriental v 54, 57, 84
Medicines, use, efficacy, nature 129
Meditation, results, 136, 139
Mind, laws, knowledge of, need 133
Muscular movements, volitional fluence, 116

Nadis, definition, 111
Navel, importance, 122–123
Nervous system—
   central, anatomical arrangen 118
   functions, 34, 35, 39–40
   government, 103
   relation to nadis, 111–113
New race, future, 151–152

Oriental practices, warning ag: 115, 129

Pancreas, secretion and func 48
Personality, nature, vehicle, 11!
Physical body, sane treatment,
Pineal gland—
   awakening and interaction pituitary, 141–142
   description and function, 41–
Pituitary gland—
   functions, 44–45
   two lobes, 141
Poise, right, importance, 135
Powers—
   eight soul, 125–126
   resulting from practice of s of soul, 137–139
Prana—
   conduction and distribution,
   effects upon form, 109
   importance in undeveloped son, 122
   oriental teaching, 93, 97–99 105, 106, 109
Psychologist, oriental, emphas position, 54–59
Psychology—
   definition, 32–33

chology—continued
:astern, concern and nature, 26–28
modern, knowledge and understanding, recommendations, 133
ew, emergence, possibility, 18
end, 90
vo systems, results, 28
vo systems, union, possibility, 28–29
'estern concern and nature, 18–26
ty of life, five rules, 135

onse apparatus, 33, 34–52

nce, situation today, 16–17
et *Doctrine,* quotation, 81–82

vareness of physical, possibility, 28
oriental psychology, 27–29
ient principle in nature, 109
· plexus centre, 48, 122

aracteristic, main, 109
ntrol by, importance, 130
ative power, 148–149
rect action on etheric body, 135
covery, 131, 133, 136–137
pression, perfect, production through mechanism, 29, 109
ictioning possibility, recognition, 71
owledge of, intellectual attainment, 134
, domination of all, 122
ation, theories, 85–89

nature, views, 72–85
picture, complete, 128–129
powers. *See* Powers.
science, technique, eight stages, 135–137
Spiritual—
achievement mode, four steps, 133–134
energy vehicle, 115
Subjective form behind objective body, 69
Substance—
definition, 56
union with life, result, 57
Sympathetic—
nerves, 117–118
system, brain of, 123

Tantric system, use, warning, 115, 129
Telepathy, dependence on etheric body, 148
Thalamus, function, 103
Thymus gland, discussion, 47–48
Thyroid gland, functions, 46–47

Universal substance, Eastern theories, 56–57, 58–59
Upanishads, doctrines, 82, 92, 93–94, 101, 102, 103

Vital body. *See* Etheric body.

Warning against dangerous use of certain oriental practices, 115, 129

NOTES

NOTES

NOTES